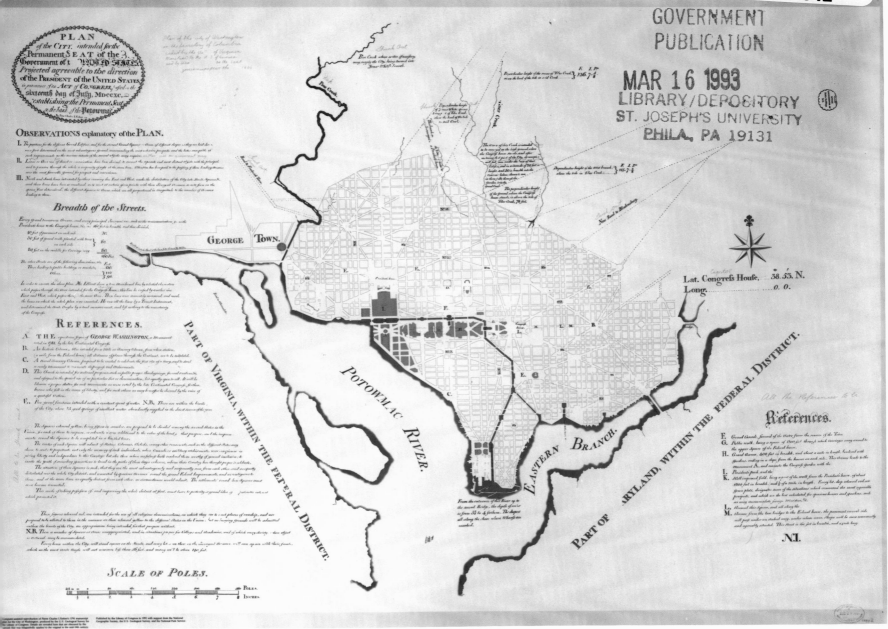

"A PLAN WHOL[L]Y NEW"

Pierre Charles L'Enfant's Plan of the City of Washington

"A PLAN WHOL[L]Y NEW"*

Pierre Charles L'Enfant's Plan of the City of Washington

By Richard W. Stephenson   *Geography and Map Division*

Library of Congress   Washington   1993

In Memory of Friend and Colleague
JAMES L. GOLLIVER
1940–1989

Library of Congress Cataloging-in-Publication Data

Stephenson, Richard W., 1930–
      A plan whol[l]y new : Pierre Charles L'Enfant's plan of
      the City of Washington / by Richard W. Stephenson.
         p.   cm.
      Includes bibliographical references and index.
      ISBN 0-8444-0699-6
---- ------ Copy 3 Z663.35 P63   1993
      1. L'Enfant, Pierre Charles, 1754–1825—Criticism and
interpretation. 2. City planning—Washington (D.C.)
I. Title.
NA9085.L47S74   1993
711'.4'0953--dc20   92-28798
                                            CIP

ENDPAPERS—
Figure 1. Computer-assisted reproduction of Pierre Charles L'Enfant's "Plan of the City, intended for the Permanent Seat of the Government of the United States," 1791. Geography and Map Division, LC.

*Title taken from a sentence in Pierre Charles L'Enfant's letter to George Washington, August 19, 1791 (14, L'Enfant Papers, oversize cabinet 2, drawer 1, Manuscript Division, LC).

For sale by the U.S. Government Printing Office, Superintendent of Documents, Mail Stop: SSOP, Washington, D.C. 20402–9328
ISBN 0-16-038220-3

CONTENTS

LIST OF ILLUSTRATIONS

FOREWORD

One of the treasures of the Library of Congress is Pierre Charles L'Enfant's original manuscript plan of the City of Washington. Compiled in 1791 at the request of George Washington and edited by Thomas Jefferson, this plan has guided the design of the nation's capital for two centuries. To commemorate its bicentennial year, 1991, the Library of Congress believed that it would be most fitting to publish two full-size facsimiles, one derived from conventional, high quality photography, the other based on the latest computer graphics technology.

This volume, designed to accompany the facsimiles, traces the fascinating history of L'Enfant's plan from its conception by Washington, Jefferson, and L'Enfant in the rustic eighteenth-century Maryland countryside to its preservation in the Library of Congress. Funded jointly by the Library of Congress and the National Geographic Society, with assistance from the U.S. Geological Survey and the U.S. Park Service, the publication of this volume and the L'Enfant plan is part of a four-year program to make the Library's premier cartographic collection of the nation's capital more accessible to researchers and at the same time preserve it for future generations.

Ralph E. Ehrenberg
Chief
Geography and Map Division

PREFACE

As I write this preface, I am reminded that it was two hundred years ago to the day that Pierre Charles L'Enfant arrived in the river port of Georgetown, Maryland, to begin planning a capital city for the United States of America. In less than a year, he prepared a plan for the city which still serves as the framework for the nation's capital. L'Enfant also compiled preliminary plans for several buildings, such as the Capitol and the President's House. The building plans were never implemented and unfortunately are no longer extant, but his ground plan of the city, submitted to President George Washington in August 1791, has survived. After many years of overuse and minimal care, this precious document was transferred to the Library of Congress on November 11, 1918, for proper storage and restoration. Today, the plan forms the cornerstone of the Library's unrivalled collection of maps and atlases of the city of Washington, D.C.

My interest in L'Enfant and his plan, as well as other maps and mapmakers associated with the City of Washington, began while I served from 1954 to 1966 as a reference librarian in the Library's Geography and Map Division, and this interest has continued unabated to this day. In 1979, I had the opportunity to write an article for *The Quarterly Journal of the Library of Congress* tracing the creation and provenance of the L'Enfant manuscript plan preserved in the Library of Congress. Entitled "The Delineation of a Grand Plan," my article was one of three in the summer 1979 issue on the subject of the L'Enfant plan and subsequent maps and plans created in the city's Surveyor's Office.

In 1987, the Library of Congress received a grant of $348,250 from the National Geographic Society which permitted the Geography and Map Division to commence an ambitious four-year program to make its Washington, D.C., map and atlas collection more readily and widely known. Key elements of this undertaking were, first, to restore or stabilize L'Enfant's manuscript so that future generations of Americans would have an opportunity to see the original plan and, second, to prepare an exact facsimile reproduction for dissemination and study. I was assigned to work on various aspects of the project including coordinating the restoration and photography of the plan and the subsequent publication of the Library's full-sized facsimile reproduction. My work with the plan afforded me the opportunity to restudy the original L'Enfant textual records and related papers in the Library's Manuscript Division and in the National Archives. The results of my study are incorporated into the essay which follows.

I wish to express my appreciation to the National Geographic Society who generously awarded the Library of Congress the money needed to undertake the Washington, D.C., Map Project, and especially to John A. Wolter and Ralph E. Ehrenberg, former Chief and Chief, respectively, of the Geography and Map Division, who were instrumental in the Library's proposing and subsequently receiving the four-year grant. They were responsible for my being involved in all aspects of the project, for which I am exceedingly grateful.

There would be no book if not for the interest shown in the project by Dana J. Pratt, the Library's director of publishing. For his support and that of his colleagues, Editor Iris Newsom and Production Manager Johanna Craig, I am most appreciative.

Special thanks are extended to Denise Gotay who assisted me in checking the quotations and verifying the notes, and for patiently inputting my entire manuscript. Also, my thanks to Carla Bussey and Tonya Tyler, Secretary and Assistant Secretary, respectively, in the Geography and Map Division, who input the final corrections and additions.

I am most grateful to Andrew J. Cosentino, Exhibits Director, Interpretive Programs Office, for having taken the time from his busy schedule to read and comment on the manuscript. An excellent editor, his comments are always most helpful.

My work in the Manuscript Division of the Library of Congress was significantly expedited by the expertise of Mary M. Wolfskill, Head of the Reference and Reader Service Section, and reference librarians Charles J. Kelly, Frederick W. Bauman, Jr., and Jeffrey M. Flannery. Their skill and good humor made it a pleasure to work in the Manuscript Reading Room.

Doris A. Hamburg, head of the Conservation Office's Paper Conservation Section, and paper conservators Heather Egan Wanser and Marian

Peck Dirda have been most helpful in matters of map conservation and especially in ensuring the safety of the fragile plan during times of transport, photography, and examination.

Finally, I wish to thank the numerous persons who have discussed L'Enfant and his plan with me over the years, especially, L'Enfant scholar Pamela Scott, architect and local historian Donald Hawkins, architect and L'Enfant expert J. L. Sibley Jennings, Jr., Washington, D.C., Public Records Administrator Philip Ogilvie; and historian Kenneth Bowling, coeditor of the Documentary History of the First Federal Congress Project.

Richard W. Stephenson
*Specialist in American
    Cartographic History
Geography and Map Division
March 9, 1991*

(Mr. Stephenson retired from the Library in January of 1992.)

"A PLAN WHOL[L]Y NEW"

*A*mong the great issues that the First Congress faced in its initial deliberations was where to locate the capital of the new nation. The Constitution of the United States (Article 1, Section 8, Clause 17) gave Congress the power "To exercise exclusive Legislation in all Cases whatsoever, over such District (not exceeding ten Miles square) as may, by Cession of particular States, and the acceptance of Congress, become the Seat of the Government of the United States."

Selecting a Site

The selection of a site was a divisive issue with much political and economic power riding on the outcome. It is little wonder then that it evoked strong state, regional, local, and personal jealousies. Powerful voices were raised both in and out of Congress in support of the leading established urban centers of Philadelphia and New York, and equally strong opinions were expressed for lesser populated places such as Annapolis and Baltimore, Maryland, Trenton, New Jersey, Wilmington, Delaware, and Reading and Lancaster, Pennsylvania to name but a few of the more than thirty places put forth in deliberations in the First Congress of the United States and its predecessor body, the Continental Congress. Debates on the subject were not limited to the houses of Congress, but were reported and editorialized in the leading papers of the day, as well as in pamphlets and broadsides.

On December 6, 1789, for example, a committee of five prominent citizens from Alexandria and five from Georgetown issued a broadside extolling the merits of locating the capital of the nation on the banks of the Potomac River. Designed to inform "the principal Towns in the Eastern States, on this interesting subject," the broadside describes the centrality of the site, the great distance inland that the river is navigable to seagoing vessels, the availability of many safe anchorages, and the ease with which the Ohio River may be reached from the headwaters of the Potomac.[1]

A second great issue facing Congress and one that had defied resolution was the payment of Revolutionary War debts. Secretary of the Treasury Alexander Hamilton had argued strongly for the assumption of the state debts by the federal government since they were incurred in a common cause. States with large debts, such as Massachusetts and South Carolina, were in favor of the federal government assuming responsibility for them; whereas states with smaller remaining debts—Virginia, for example—did not. With the exception of South Carolina, the southern states were against the measure.[2] These two great issues facing Congress were eventually to be joined and resolved together.

The Compromise

Public interest in a permanent seat of government had been whetted by numerous debates in Congress over finding a site that would be acceptable to Northern, Middle, and Southern interests. The issue was finally resolved at a dinner in June 1790 in which Secretary of State Thomas Jefferson invited Alexander Hamilton and Representative James Madison of Virginia to be his guests. At this momentous dinner the issues were discussed at length, but before a compromise could be struck, "it was observed, I forget by which of them," Jefferson later wrote, "that as the pill would be a bitter one to the Southern states, something should be done to soothe them; that the removal of the seat of government to the Patowmac was a just measure, & would probably be a popular one with them, and would be a proper one to follow the assumption."[3] Madison agreed to support Hamilton's plan to have the federal government assume the debts incurred by the colonies during the American Revolutionary War and the temporary location of the capital in Philadelphia in exchange for Hamilton's support in permanently locating the federal district on the banks of the Potomac River by the year 1800.

With Hamilton's successful behind-the-scene maneuvering, the establishment and general location of the federal territory was agreed upon by Congress with the passage of "An Act for establishing the temporary and permanent seat of the Government of the United States."[4] Signed into law on July 16, 1790, the act established "a district of territory, not exceeding ten miles square, to be located, as hereafter directed on the river Potomac, at some place between the mouths of the Eastern Branch and Connogochegue," with the selection of the actual site being left to the President.[5]

True to his word, Madison successfully delivered the votes needed for the passage of the funding bill containing a provision for the assumption of state debts. With the successful conclusion of the "Compromise of 1790," as it has been called, Congress averted a national disaster. "The Constitution survived its first major crisis," wrote historian Kenneth R. Bowling, "because of the willingness of the American public to accept the compromise worked out by the executive and legislative branches of the federal government in 1790. The first publicly fought compromise in American history, it marked the end of the American Revolution, for it resolved the two most difficult and lingering issues: payment of the war debt and the location of the capital."[6]

Initial Planning

President Washington, ever fearful of Philadelphia interests attempting to repeal the Residence Act, moved as quickly as his official duties would permit to implement the new legislation. His first order of business was to determine the most suitable place for the Federal Territory along the sixty-six-mile stretch of the Potomac River specified by the Residence Act.

In late August, Secretary of State Jefferson began to formulate some thoughts for the President's consideration concerning the structure of the capital city. The streets, he proposed, should "be at right angles as in Philadelphia, & that no street be narrower than 100. feet, with foot-ways [i.e., sidewalks] of 15. feet. Where a street is long & level [i.e., avenues and boulevards], it might be 120. feet wide."[7] Each square or block in the city, he suggested, be "at least 200. yards every way, which will be of about 8. acres each."[8]

Jefferson even conceived of a unique method of dividing each square into lots, illustrating his suggestion with a tiny sketch (Figure 2). Each lot he envisioned would measure fifty feet in width at the street with "their depths to extend to the diagonal of the square."[9]

Jefferson also questioned the practice in many cities of requiring all houses to be built at a uniform distance from the street. "It produces a disgusting monotony," he opinioned, noting that "all persons make this complaint against Philadelphia."[10]

The Secretary of State also favored the eventual enactment of legislation aimed at restricting the height of buildings, pointing out that "In Paris it is forbidden to build a house beyond a given height, & it is admitted to be a good restriction. it keeps down the prices of ground, keeps the houses low & convenient, & the streets

When the President shall have made up his mind as to the spot for the town, would there be any impropriety in his saying to the neighboring landholders, "I will fix the town here if you will join & purchase & give the lands." they may well afford it from the increase of value it will give to their own circumjacent lands.

The lots to be sold out in breadth of 50. feet: their depths to extend to the diagonal of the square.

I doubt much whether the obligation to build the houses at a given distance from the street, contributes to it's beauty. it produces a disgusting monotony. all persons make this complaint against Philadelphia. the contrary practice varies the appearance, & is much more convenient to the inhabitants.

In Paris it is forbidden to build a house beyond a given height & it is admitted to be a good restriction. it keeps down the price of ground, keeps the houses low & convenient, & the streets light & airy. fires are much more manageable where houses are low.

light & airy, fires are much more manageable where houses are low."[11]

On the way to their homes in central Virginia in September 1790, Jefferson and Madison stopped at the small river port of Georgetown, Maryland, situated below the falls of the Potomac River. Here they held discussions with several prominent citizens concerning the location and establishment of a capital city. They reported to the President, then at home in nearby Mount Vernon, that they had met with a local land-owner, probably George Mason who owned substantial land along the Potomac River in Virginia, including Analostan or Mason's Island opposite Georgetown.[12] Although reluctant to speak at first, Mason subsequently urged that the capital be built in the vicinity of Georgetown, Maryland. To support his argument for this location, Mason noted that "1. It's being at the junction of the upper & lower navigation where the commodities must be transferred into other vessels: . . . 2. the depth of water which would admit any vessels that could come to Alexandria. 3. the narrowness of the river & consequent safeness of the harbour. 4. it's being clear of ice as early at least as

the canal & river above would be clear. 5. it's neighborhood to the Eastern branch, whither any vessels might conveniently withdraw which should be detained through the winter. 6. it's defensibility, as derived from the high & commanding hills around it. 7. it's actual possession of the commerce, & the start it already has."[13]

Notes prepared by Jefferson at this time, probably for use in discussions with the President, indicate his concern for finding a suitable method for financing the construction of the new city. He describes conversations he had with three residents from Georgetown identified by Jefferson as "Mr. Carrol, Mr. Stoddard and Mr. Dickens" (i.e., Daniel Carroll of Rock Creek, Benjamin Stoddert, and William Deakins, Jr.) in which he suggested that if the local proprietors wanted the capital city to be located on their lands, they should agree to "give them up for the use of the U.S. on condition they should receive the double of their value, estimated as they would have been had there been no thought of bringing the federal seat into their neighborhood." As an alternative method, Jefferson "suggested as more certain means of ensuring the object, that each proprietor within the whole ten miles square, should cede one half his lands to the public, to be sold to raise money." He concluded, however, that "perhaps this would

-pleating the 10. miles in that direction, which will bring the lower boundary on the Maryland side very nearly opposite to P t on the Virginia side. ― It is understood that the breadth of the territory accepted will be of 5. miles only on each side.

2. in locating the town, will it not be best to give it double the extent on the eastern branch of what it has on the river? the former will be for persons in commerce, the latter for those connected with the government.

3. will it not be best to lay out the long streets parallel with the creek, and the other crossing them at right angles, so as to leave no oblique angled lots but the single row which shall be on the river? thus.

creek

6

be pushing them too far for the reputation of the new government they were to come under."[14]

It is also clear from his comments that he had in mind a small Federal city of some 1500 acres, with "300 acres for public buildings, walks &c and 1200 acres to be divided into quarter acre lots, which, due allowance being made for streets, would make about 2000 lots." To start with, Jefferson thought that the city would need public buildings and "about 20 good dwelling houses for such persons belonging to the government as must have houses to themselves, about as many good lodging houses, and half a dozen taverns."[15]

Jefferson also included in his notes a small sketch of a proposed federal city consisting of thirty-four squares laid out in a rectangular pattern.[16] His rough sketch (Figure 3) closely resembles the town of Carrollsburg laid out in 1770 on land belonging to Charles Carroll of Duddington situated at the confluence of the Eastern Branch with the Potomac River. Although its lots were disposed of by lottery, Carrollsburg never developed as a viable river port and remained largely a "paper town" (Figure 4).

Figure 3. Thomas Jefferson's plan for a federal city at the junction of the Eastern Branch with the Potomac River, September 14, 1790. Jefferson's sketch resembles the plan of Carrollsburg laid out in 1770. *Manuscript Division, LC.*

Concerning his sketch, Jefferson posed the following questions:

2. in locating the town, will it not be best to give it double the extent on the eastern branch of what it has on the river? the former will be for persons in commerce, the latter for those connected with the government.
3. will it not be best to lay out the long streets parallel with the creek, and the other crossing them at right angles, so as to leave no oblique angled lots but the single row which shall be on the river?[17]

The President Chooses a Site

Washington journeyed to Georgetown, Maryland, for a personal inspection of the site. The Georgetown weekly, *The Times, and Patowmack Packet*, reported that on October 16, the President "in Company with the principal Gentlemen of this town and neighbourhood, set out to view the Country adjacent to the River Patowmack, in order to fix upon a proper situation for the Grand Columbian Federal City."[18] Nine of the local landowners had written to the President three days earlier (as suggested by the Secretary of State) offering to make their property available "should their Lands, or any part of them be selected for the Federal City," pointing out that "no place in the small distance from the mouth of the Eastern Branch, to the highest Tide Water, offers so many advantages—and that to none

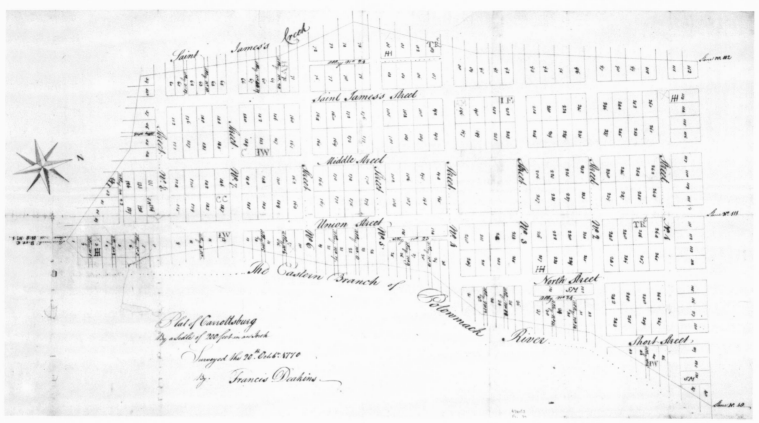

Figure 4. Francis Deakins' "Plat of Carrollsburg" surveyed on October 20, 1770. The map is oriented with north to the right. *Geography and Map Division, LC.*

there can be so few solid objections as to George Town and its immediate vicinity."[19]

After the warm welcome President Washington received from the citizens of Georgetown and environs, he proceeded on his planned tour of the area north of the Falls of the Potomac in search of other suitable sites. Local politicians, merchants, and landowners in the northern reaches of the region, especially Washington County, Maryland, enthusiastically supported the undertaking and encouraged the President to locate the federal seat in their locale. Washington, however, returned to Mount Vernon and thence to Philadelphia without making a public statement as to his choice for the federal city, wisely hoping that competition within the region would lead to the government acquiring the needed land under the most favorable conditions possible.

Speculation persisted that President Washington would soon announce his decision and that it would be the area he knew best—the environs of Georgetown, Maryland, and Alexandria, Virginia. Merchant Samuel Davidson's comments written to Robert Dunlop in London on November 28, are probably representative of the opinions then prevalent in the Georgetown business community:

> We have not now a doubt remaining, but that the Grand Federal City will soon rear its August head in the vicinity of this Town—the President has fixed upon the place, altho not yet certainly known—his Speech to Congress, on the first monday in December, will reveal the Secret; in the mean time, if you have any confidence in my judgement, you may calculate that, from Rock Creek to the Eastern Branch is the place; and say, that on the hights [sic] of Peter's *Slashes* Plantation, will stand the Stadt [i.e., State] House.[20]

The President, however, did not publicly settle the issue until the new year. On January 22, 1791, he appointed Daniel Carroll and Thomas Johnson from the State of Maryland, and David Stuart from Virginia, all prominent citizens and trusted friends, to serve as Commissioners for the Federal District. Daniel Carroll of Rock Creek (1730–1796) lived in what is today Forest Glen, a short distance from the District line in Montgomery County, Maryland. At the time of his appointment, he was serving his state as a representative to the First Congress. He was an uncle of Daniel Carroll of Duddington, the largest landholder in the area subsequently selected for the new city. Thomas Johnson (1732–1819), whose home was in Frederick, Maryland, some forty-three miles northwest of Georgetown, served as a member of the Continental Congress, first governor of the state of Maryland, and associate justice of the U.S. Supreme Court. Along with George Washington, he was instrumental in organizing the Potowmack Company in 1785 to improve navigation on the Potomac River. Dr. David Stuart

(1753–1811) was a practicing physician whose estate, Hope Park, was in nearby Fairfax County, Virginia. Stuart was not only a close friend of the President, but had married the widow of Martha Washington's son, John Parke Custis.[21] Working under his direction, the Commissioners were empowered to "survey, and by proper metes and bounds define and limit a district of territory."[22] In addition, they were authorized "to purchase or accept such quantity of land on the eastern side of the said river [i.e., Potomac], within the said district, as the President shall deem proper for the use of the United States."[23]

Two days later, the President issued a proclamation noting that "after duly examining & weighing the advantages & disadvantages of the several situations" he had decided to place the ten-mile-square Federal Territory on the banks of the Potomac River in the environs of Georgetown.[24] In forwarding a copy of the proclamation to Congress, the President requested that the Residence Act be amended so that the Federal Territory would "comprehend the Eastern branch itself, & some of the Country on its lower side in the state of Maryland, & the town of Alexandria in Virginia."[25] Washington had come to believe that the potential value of the Eastern Branch for commerce and shipping was so great that both sides of the river should be included in the Federal Territory. Congress gave its approval to this request on March 3, 1791.

The Geographical Setting

The one-hundred-square-mile Federal Territory chosen by the President was situated at the head of tidewater navigation on the Potomac River ninety-six miles from its confluence with the Chesapeake Bay. Oceangoing vessels then navigated the Potomac and its tributary, the Eastern Branch. Further navigation upstream on the Potomac by large vessels was barred due to the descent of the river from the higher elevation of the Piedmont or foothills of the Blue Ridge Mountains to the Atlantic coastal plain through a narrow gorge creating the formidable Great and Little Falls. The Eastern Branch, whose name was soon to be changed to the Anacostia River, in honor of the native Indians that formerly lived on its banks, was navigable to the town of Bladensburg, Maryland, seven and a half miles upstream.

Other streams flowing into the Potomac included Four-Mile Run and Spout Run on the Virginia side and Rock Creek, St. James Creek, and Goose Creek in Maryland. Although the latter name was used by local residents throughout most of the eighteenth century, with the establishment of the Federal Territory the preferred name became Tiber Creek, a name borrowed from Rome and considered by supporters of the new venture to be more in keeping with the image of a capital city of a great nation.[26] Tiber Creek rose on the higher land in the northern part of the Federal Territory, descended southwestwardly to sea level at the western foot of Jenkins' Hill (later called Capitol Hill) and then sluggishly flowed westward through tidewater flats and marshland into the Potomac River. This creek, draining 2600 acres or 43 percent of the land that was to be laid out for the city, was to figure prominently in early transportation and beautification plans.[27]

The Federal Territory was a long and well-settled area consisting of the existing river ports of Georgetown, Maryland, immediately below the head of navigation, and Alexandria, Virginia, six and a half miles downstream, as well as the largely undeveloped towns of Carrollsburg and Hamburg on the Maryland side. Most of the acreage, however, consisted of woodland and farms on which tobacco, wheat, and corn were grown.

The site within the Federal Territory selected by the President for laying out the new city was a broad, triangular-shaped 6111-acre parcel of land rising from the Potomac River and the Eastern Branch in a series of four steplike terraces.

Tobias Lear, President Washington's secretary, noted that "The ground, on an average, is about forty feet above water of the river. Although the whole, when taken together, appears to be nearly a level spot, yet it is found to consist of what may be called wavy land; and is sufficiently uneven to give many very extensive and beautiful views from various parts of it, as well as to effectually answer every purpose of cleansing and draining the city."[28]

The site for the new city was crossed by the Georgetown-Ferry Road (approximating Pennsylvania Avenue today), the Bladensburg-Ferry Road, a road from the Potomac River Ferry to Bladensburg-Ferry Road, and a road from Rock Creek Church to the Eastern Branch. Routes leading to and from the city site included the Alexandria-Georgetown Road which crossed the Potomac at Mason's Ferry, the Georgetown-Bladensburg Road, part of which subsequently served as the northwest boundary of the new city, Rock Creek Church Road, and the Georgetown-Frederick Road (Figure 5).

The Appointment of Ellicott and L'Enfant

With the appointment of the three commissioners and the issuance of a public announcement describing his choice for the location of the

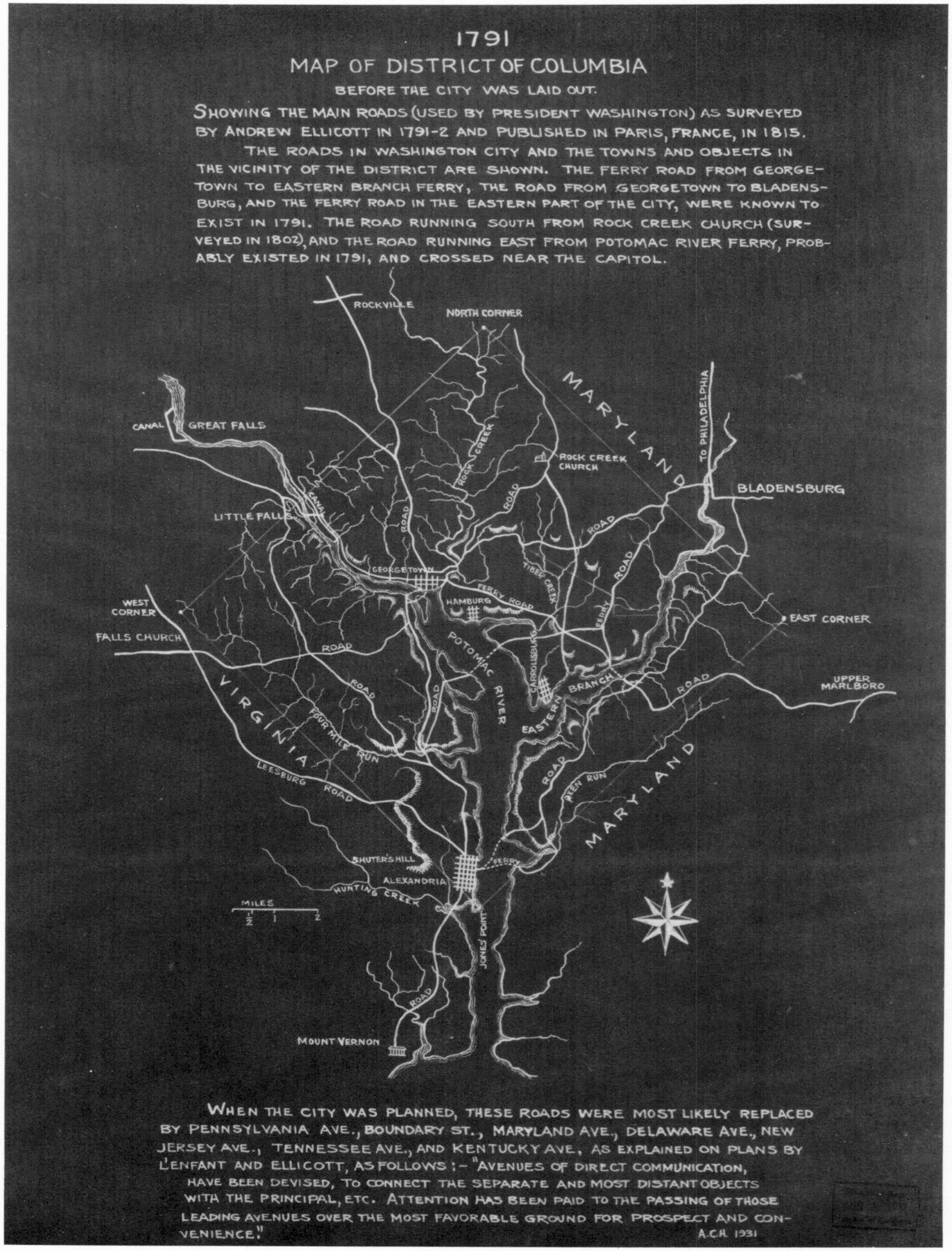

Figure 5. Artemas C. Harmon's map showing the main roads in existence before the city of Washington was laid out in 1791. *Geography and Map Division, LC.*

Federal Territory, the President now turned his attention to surveying and mapping the site and preparing a plan for the capital city. For the undertaking he chose Andrew Ellicott, one of the nation's leading surveyors and astronomers, and Pierre Charles L'Enfant, a former comrade in arms and now a practicing New York City architect (Figure 6).

Nearly a year and a half earlier, L'Enfant wrote to Washington "to sollicit the favor of being Employed in this Business" of designing the new city. Eager to "share in the undertaking," he pointed out to the President that "No nation perhaps had ever before the opportunity offerd [sic] them of deliberately deciding on the spot where thier [sic] Capital city should be fixed, or of combining every necessary consideration in the choice of situation." L'Enfant already perceived "that the plan should be drawn on such a scale as to leave room for that aggrandisement & embellishment which the increase of the wealth of the Nation will permit it to pursue at any period how ever remote." In this same letter, L'Enfant also sought "the appointment of Engineer to the United States," pointing out to the President "that the sciences of military and civil architecture are so connected to render an Engineer Equally serviceable in time of peace as in war by the employment of his abilities in the internal improvemen[t] of the Country."[29]

Figure 6. Silhouette of Pierre L'Enfant by Sarah DeHart, ca. 1785. It is part of a collage assembled by DeHart containing other silhouettes, drawings, music, and poems. *Reproduced courtesy of the Diplomatic Reception Rooms, U.S. Department of State.*

Born in Paris on August 2, 1754, L'Enfant was the son of Pierre L'Enfant, an artist known for his landscapes and battle scenes and a "Painter in Ordinary to the King in his manufacture of the Gobelin tapestries."[30] L'Enfant received his education at the Royal Academy of Painting and Sculpture where his father served as an instructor. Caught up in the spirit of the American Revolutionary War, L'Enfant, at the age of twenty-two, volunteered to serve with the Continental Army. He spent the winter of 1777–1778 at Valley Forge, Pennsylvania. On February 18, 1778, he was commissioned Captain of Engineers and attached to the staff of Inspector General Baron Friedrich von Steuben. L'Enfant subsequently moved to the southern theater of war where in October 1779 he participated gallantly in the abortive seige of Savannah. L'Enfant was wounded while attempting to set fire to a British position. A few months later, while still recovering from the wound, he was taken captive at the fall of Charleston, South Carolina. L'Enfant remained a prisoner of war until January 1782 when he was exchanged for German captive Lieutenant de Heyden of the Anspach Yägers. On May 2, 1783, L'Enfant was promoted to Brevet Major in the Corps of Engineers.[31]

As a former officer in the U.S. Army, he became a member of the newly established Society of the Cincinnati. His artistic training being well known to the members, L'Enfant was asked to design the insignia and certificate of the Society. These he had executed in Paris in 1783–1784. L'Enfant returned to America in 1784 and established himself in New York City as an architect. He is best remembered for his role in converting New York City's old City Hall on Wall Street into Federal Hall (Figure 7). It was here that George Washington was inaugurated as the first President of the United States on April 30, 1789.

L'Enfant was an artist and architect of great talent, with some practical knowledge in engineering acquired during his service with the American army. His multifaceted abilities were recognized by Washington and others who considered him ideally suited for the task of laying out a new city. The banker and philanthropist William W. Corcoran described L'Enfant as "a tall, erect man, fully six feet in height, finely proportioned, nose prominent, of military bearing, courtly air and polite manners, his figure usually enveloped in a long overcoat and surmounted by a bell-crowned hat—a man who would attract attention in any assembly."[32] His colleague on the project, Andrew Ellicott, told his wife that "he is a most worthy French gentleman and tho' not one of the most handsome of men, he is from his good breeding, and native politeness, a first rate favorite among the la-

Figure 7. Federal Hall, New York City, was redesigned by L'Enfant for the inauguration of George Washington. Lithograph after an engraving by Cornelius Tiebout. *Prints and Photographs Division, LC.*

dies."[33] Before the undertaking was completed, however, L'Enfant's inability to compromise, his failure to grasp the political realities of the situation, and perhaps his artistic temperament were to prove his undoing.

Instructions for the Surveyor and the City Planner

On February 2, Jefferson requested Ellicott "to proceed by the first stage to the Federal territory on the Potomac, for the purpose of making a survey of it." He was instructed to survey the lines of Territory, the first two of which "must run with all the accuracy of which your art is susceptible as they are to fix the beginning either on Hunting Creek or the River." He was also to "note the position of the mouth of the Eastern Branch," "the position of George-town, and mouth of Goose Creek," and place this information on a plat and send it by post to the President as soon as possible. Then, while waiting for additional instructions, he was to ascertain "a true Meridian, and the latitude of the place, and running the meanderings of the Eastern Branch, and of the River itself, and other waters which will merit an exact place in the map of the Territory."[34]

One month later, Secretary of State Jefferson requested L'Enfant to proceed to the Federal Territory and begin preparations for a ground plan of the likely site for the capital city. L'Enfant had previously been contacted by Commissioner Daniel Carroll of Rock Creek and formally asked to participate in the undertaking.[35] Jefferson carefully instructed L'Enfant to begin his reconnaissance "on the Eastern branch and proceed from thence upwards, laying down the hills, vallies, morasses, and waters between that, the Potomac, the Tyber, and the road leading from George Town to the Eastern branch, and connecting the whole with certain fixed points of the map Mr. Ellicott is preparing."[36]

L'Enfant was unaware that his instructions were in part a ploy designed to make the George-town landowners think that the principal part of the new city was to be built on the lands of Daniel Carroll of Duddington in the vicinity of the Eastern Branch. Earlier, Washington had written to his trusted agents, William Deakins, Jr. and Benjamin Stoddert, requesting them to purchase several critical parcels of land for the city at a reasonable rate. "The object of this letter," the President noted, "is to ask you to endeavor to purchase these grounds of the owners for the public, . . . but as if for yourselves, and to conduct your propositions so as to excite no suspicion that they are on behalf of the public."[37] The President informed Deakins and Stoddert one month later that L'Enfant would soon arrive in Georgetown to survey the land "within the

Eastern branch, the Potowmac, the Tyber, & the road leading from George town to the ferry on the Eastern branch he is directed to begin at the lower end and work upwards, & *nothing further is communicated to him."* Washington was taking no chances that his agents would be "misled by this appearance, nor be diverted from the pursuit of the objects I have recommended to you. I expect that your progress in accomplishing them will be facilitated by the presumption which will arise on seeing this operation begun at the Eastern branch, & that the proprietors nearer George town who have hitherto refused to accommodate, will let themselves down to reasonable terms."[38]

Washington and Jefferson had decided that if Deakins and Stoddert were successful in obtaining the necessary land, the new city would be built adjacent to Georgetown. It would extend from Rock Creek to the mouth of the Tiber and incorporate the lands of the previously platted town of Hamburg. This is confirmed by Jefferson's draft of the proclamation issued by the President on March 30 describing the amended boundaries of the Federal Territory and directing the Commissioners "to proceed forthwith to have the sd [i.e., said] four lines run." Jefferson's draft includes the following lines not incorporated into the published version:

> And Whereas the sd first mentioned act of Congress did further enact that the sd Commissioners should, under the direction of the President of the U.S. provide suitable buildings for the accommodation of Congress & of the President & for the public offices of the government of the United States, I do hereby further declare and make known, that [the highest summit of lands in the town heretofore called Hamburg, within the sd territory, with a convenient extent of grounds circumjacent, shall be appropriated for a Capitol for the accommodation of Congress, & such other lands between Georgetown & the stream heretofore called the Tyber, as shall on due examination be found convenient & sufficient, shall be appropriated for the accommodation of the President of the U.S. for the time being, & for the public offices of the government of the U.S.]

Jefferson added a note that "The part within [] being conjectural, will be rendered conformable to the ground when more accurately examined."[39]

Jefferson Draws a Plan

Washington and Jefferson's ideas for the location and general layout of the new city are embodied in a sketch map prepared by the latter in March 1791.[40] The site chosen incorporated the townsite of Hamburg (Figure 8). Laid out in 1768 into 234 lots by Jacob Funk of Frederick, Maryland, by 1791 Hamburg remained little more than a paper town. Hamburg or Funkstown, as it was sometimes called, was situated on the shore of the Potomac from what eventually became 19th to 23rd Streets, N.W. and inland to H

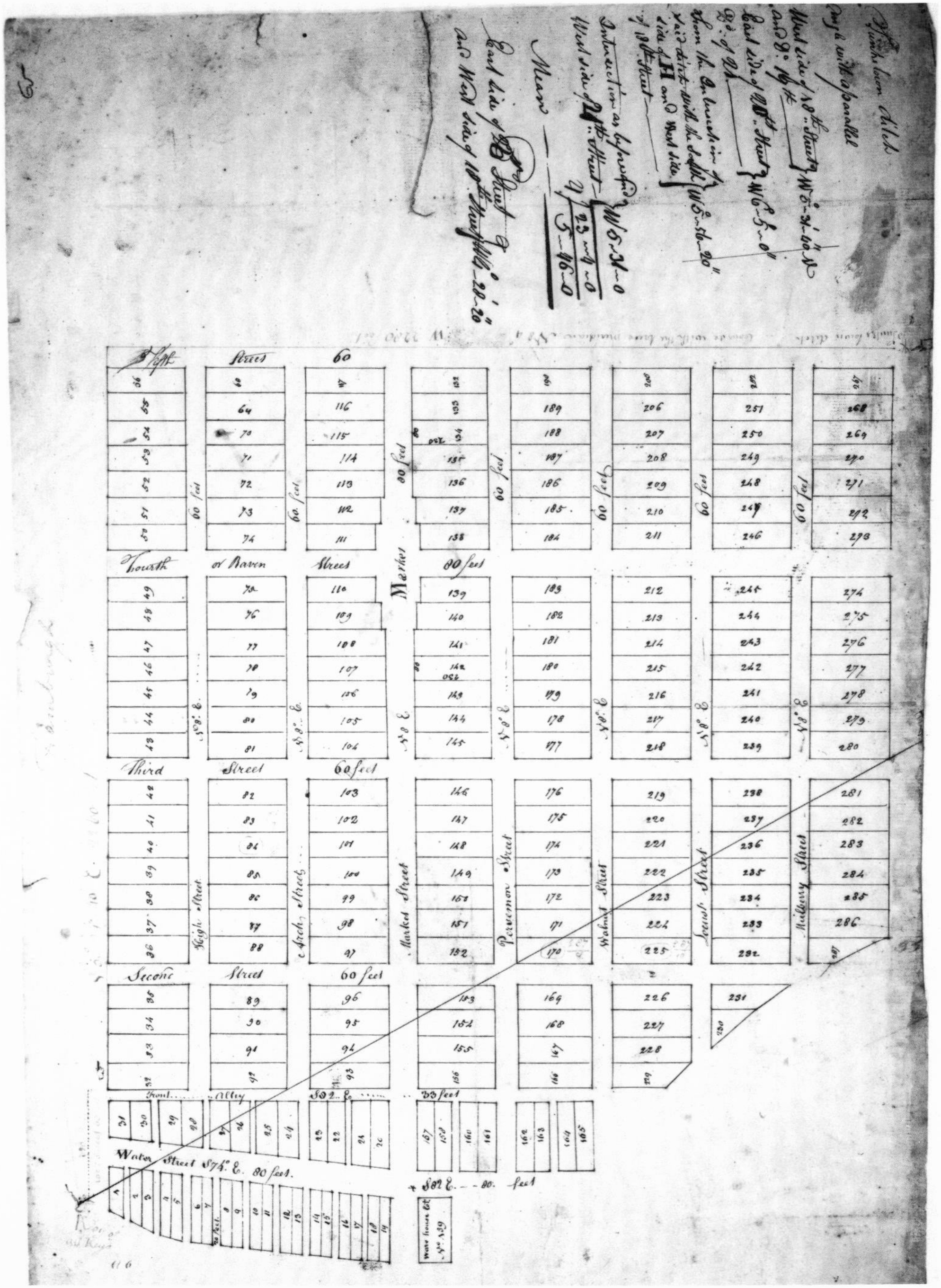

Figure 8. Plan of the town of Hamburg, later part of Washington, D.C., laid out in 1768. *Geography and Map Division, LC.*

Street, N.W. Funk had envisioned his town as a river port centered around what he hoped would be a thriving market and tobacco warehouse.

Jefferson's fascinating plan shows a modest town laid out in a checkerboard pattern on the north banks of Tiber Creek and the Potomac River and superimposed over the boundaries of Hamburg (Figure 9). Consisting of only three rows of squares running north and south and eleven rows east and west, it depicts the President's House to the west and the Capitol to the east, with "public walks" connecting the two buildings. This same spatial relationship reappears later in L'Enfant's plan, but on a much grander scale and with the nation's two principal government buildings joined by a "well improved field" (i.e., Mall) and a "Grand Avenue 400 feet in breadth."[41] Surrounding Jefferson's 273-acre capital city are a series of dots representing the corners of squares "to be laid off in future." A dashed line, unidentified in the sketch, represents a portion of the Ferry Road connecting Georgetown with the Eastern Branch. Jefferson also included water depths in the Potomac River, apparently reflecting Washington's and his continuing desire to make the new city not only a political capital, but a commercial capital as well. Jefferson traced the outline of his map from the survey made in 1790 by Charles Beatty and Archibald Orme, rough pencil copies of which

are on file in the Library's Geography and Map Division.[42]

The Arrival of Ellicott and L'Enfant

The arrival in February of Ellicott and his assistant, the black astronomer Benjamin Banneker, and L'Enfant's arrival in March did not go unnoticed, as in the extended reference to them in the March 12th issue of *The Georgetown Weekly Ledger*:

Some time last month arrived in this town Mr. *Andrew Ellicott*, a gentleman of superior astronomical abilities. He was employed by the President of the United States of America, to lay off a tract of land, ten miles square, on the Potowmack, for the use of Congress;—is now engaged in this business, and hopes soon to accomplish the object of his mission. He is attended by *Benjamin Banniker*, an Ethiopian, whose abilities, as a surveyor, and an astronomer, clearly prove that Mr. Jefferson's concluding that race of men were void of mental endowments was without foundation.

Wednesday evening arrived in this town, Major *Longfont*, a French gentleman employed by the President of the United States to survey the lands contiguous to George-Town, where the federal city is to be built. His skill in matters of this nature is justly extolled by all disposed to give merit its proper tribute of praise. He is earnest in the business, and hopes to be able to lay a plat, of that parcel of land, before the President, upon his arrival in this town.[43]

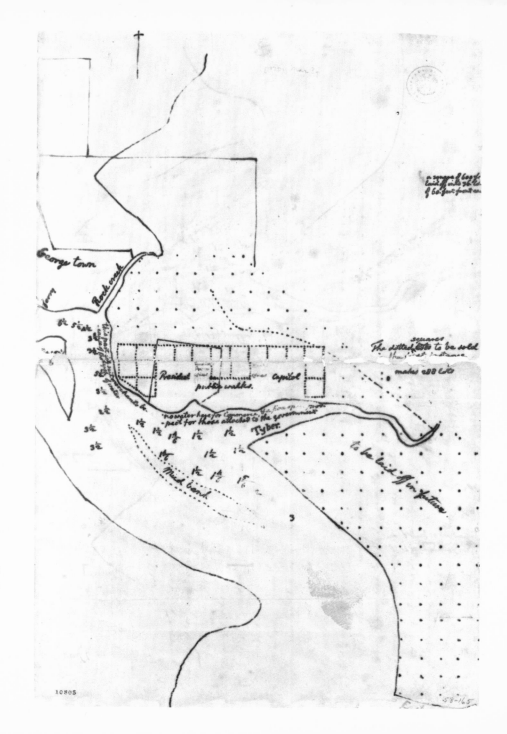

Figure 9. Thomas Jefferson's plan for a federal city on the site of Hamburg, March 1791. *Manuscript Division, LC.*

The Surveyor and the City Planner Begin Their Field Work

Ellicott began his survey of the boundary of the Federal Territory only to find that "the second line does not touch any part of Hunting Creek." He recommended that "in order to make the plan as complete as possible it will be proper to begin the survey of the ten miles square at the Eastern inclination of the upper cape of Hunting Creek [i.e., Jones Point], marked on the plat. This plan," which he forwarded to Jefferson for the President's consideration, "will include all the Harbor and wharfs of Alexandria, which will not be the Case if the two first lines mentioned in the proclamation are to remain as now."[44] This suggestion was subsequently accepted by Washington, and Jones Point became the starting point of the ten-mile-square boundary of the Territory.

Wretched weather conditions prevailed when L'Enfant arrived in Georgetown on March 9 to begin his assignment. He warned Jefferson that "Should the weather continu bad as there is Every apparence it will I shall be much at a loss how to make a plan of the ground you have pointed out to me and have it ready for the President at the time when he his [i.e., is] Expected at this place."[45] Despite the rain and fog, however, L'Enfant rode over the area on horseback and his creative mind quickly grasped the potential for a capital city that the geographical setting offered. "As far as I was able to juge through a thick Fog," L'Enfant wrote in this initial letter to Jefferson, "I passed on many spots which appeared to me realy beautiful and which seem to disput with each other who command."[46] He found the area between Ferry Road, the Potomac River and Goose or Tiber Creek to be level presenting "a situation most advantageous to run streets and prolong them on grand and Far distant point of view."[47] The broken nature of the terrain nearest Georgetown, however, appeared to him "to be less commendable for the establessement of a city." Not only was there a lack of level land, but L'Enfant felt that the area was dominated by the "heights from behind george town."[48]

Upon receiving L'Enfant's letter of March 11, Jefferson responded with new and urgent instructions. He was now to add to his delineation of the land in the environs of the Eastern Branch, "a drawing also of the principal lineaments of the ground between Rock creek & the Tyber." Furthermore, Jefferson requested that if the courses of these creeks and the Potomac River had not already been laid down, "that Mr. Ellicot should immediately do this while you shall be employed on the interior ground." The President was to be in Georgetown within a few days, Jefferson noted, and "would wish to have [the map] under his eye."[49]

The postscript to this letter is interesting because here for first time Jefferson explains the President's strategy.

> P.S. There are certainly considerable advantages on the Eastern branch: but there are very strong reasons also in favor of the position between Rock creek & Tyber independant of the face of the ground. It is the desire that the public mind should be in equilibrio between these two places till the President arrives, and we shall be obliged to you to endeavor to poise [i.e., balance] their expectations.[50]

Plagued by continued bad weather, L'Enfant struggled to complete a preliminary plan for the President's anticipated arrival. He reported to Jefferson, however, that Ellicott would "join his Endeavour to mine in runing as much as possible of the wather [i.e., water] course as may serve [to] connect the whole of our differents surveys together."[51]

L'Enfant's First Meeting with the President

Washington arrived in Georgetown on March 28, and previous to a dinner in his honor hosted by the Mayor and the town corporation, he met with Ellicott and L'Enfant to review their surveys.[52] L'Enfant struggled to get his map ready for the occasion, but it still "remained unfinished at the moment of the President['s] arrival at this place."[53] Nevertheless, L'Enfant took full advantage of the opportunity to meet face-to-face with Washington and not only displayed his rough pencil drawing of the ground, but presented him with a remarkable document describing his impressions of the landscape and his initial suggestions for improvements.[54]

L'Enfant pointed out that the land near the Eastern Branch (Southeast Washington today) was ideal "for the First Setlement of a gra[nd] City," and the Eastern Branch itself offered excellent facilities for "an harbor in Every respect to be prefered to that of the potowmack toward Georgetown."[55] In addition, he noted that the city's communication with the northern and southern states would be vastly improved with bridges over the Eastern Branch above Evans Point and the Potomac River above Georgetown.[56] If this was accomplished then attention should be paid immediately to opening "a direct & large avenue from the bridge on the potowmack to that on the Eastern branch . . . with a midle way paved for heavy carriage and walks on each side planted with double Rows of trees."[57] Such a street, "proportioned to the Greatnes which a City the Capitale of a powerfull Empire ought to manifest," would encourage development and growth "begining the Setlement of the Grand City on the bank of the eastern branch and promoting the first improvement all along of the Heigh flat."[58] L'Enfant incorporated the bridges into the plan for the city he submitted to the President in August 1791, with the important linking road subsequently being named Pennsylvania Avenue.

L'Enfant noted that since it was likely that the city would extend over a large area (from Georgetown to the Eastern Branch), "much deliberation is necessary For to determine on a plan for the local distribution and conceive that plan on a sisteem which" would be "agreable to the first Settler in it," but also "may be capable of being made a part of the whole when Enlarged by progressive Improvement."[59] In other words, the plan should be comprehensive in area and scope, thus permitting initial settlement to meld smoothly with later development.

He called the President's attention to a ridge running westward from Jenkins' Hill (Capitol Hill today) and paralleling the Potomac River that included many of the most desirable sites for the erection of "publiques Edifices there on." From this ridge, "Every grand building would rear with a majestick aspect over the Country all round and might be advantageously seen From twenty miles off."[60]

L'Enfant also expressed in this report his dislike for the gridiron pattern of streets found in most eighteenth-century American cities. "Such regular plan in deed however answerable as they may appear upon paper or seducing as they may be on the first aspect to the ayes [i.e., eyes] of some people most [i.e., must] even when applayed [i.e., applied] upon that ground the best calculated to admit of it become at last tiresome and insipide."[61] L'Enfant's answer to this design problem was to overlay the standard grid pattern with radiating avenues connecting distant points with the center of the city and "to the passing of those leading Avenues over the most favorable ground for prospect and convenience."[62]

L'Enfant's application of radiating avenues leading to significant focal points in his design for the new city may have been suggested by his personal knowledge of their use in Paris and Versailles.

Perhaps L'Enfant's innate sensitivity to the geography of the site rather than his knowledge of eighteenth-century French urban design, however, was of greater influence in the creation of his plan. "A study of L'Enfant's plan, as well as a careful reading of his descriptions," noted William T. Partridge in the National Capital Park and Planning Commission's 1930 annual report, "shows the effort made to mold his design to the existing topography. No mention can be found of Versailles or London as an inspiration. He reiterates again and again in his letters that this plan of his was 'original' and 'unique.' "[63]

The President was apparently pleased with L'Enfant's rough plan of the ground and his detailed report. L'Enfant reported to Jefferson a few days later that Washington ordered "the survey to be continued and the deliniation of a grand plan for the local distribution of the City to be done on principle conformable to the ideas which I took the liberty to hold before him as the proper for the Establishement."[64] Washington's meeting with Ellicott and L'Enfant and the events of the next two days radically changed his opinion of the size and scope of the new city.

An Agreement Is Reached with the Proprietors

Early the next morning (March 29), the President in the company of the Commissioners attempted to make a personal inspection of the site for the proposed city. The weather was so poor, however, that Washington, who earlier in his life had been a professional surveyor, remarked that he "derived no great satisfaction from the review."[65] The main issue facing the President, however, was not the topographical setting itself, but rather how to get the local proprietors to agree to make their lands available for the undertaking at a reasonable price. Washington was quite concerned over the heated dispute that had arisen between the owners of land adjacent to Georgetown and those near the Eastern Branch concerning the site for the new city and especially the location of the public buildings. At a meeting requested by the President for later in the day, he told the proprietors "that the contention in which they seemed engaged, did not in my opinion, comport either with the public interest or that of their own; that while each party was aiming to obtain the public buildings, they might, by placing the matter on a contracted scale, defeat the measure altogether."[66] He pointed out to them that neither the Georgetown nor the Carrollsburg areas individually provided sufficient space for the city he wished to have laid out. It is unclear if the President had this in the back of his mind when he arrived in Georgetown or if he changed his opinion after talking with L'Enfant and perhaps others. Nevertheless, now he informed the proprietors "That both together did not comprehend more ground nor would afford greater means than was required for the federal City."[67] He urged the landowners, therefore, to put aside their dispute and "make a common cause of it and thereby secure it to the district."[68] He was now committed to what L'Enfant referred to as a city drawn on a "grand plan."[69]

Washington's prestige and his powers of persuasion worked; the next day, nineteen property owners agreed with him that "whilst they were contending for the shadow they might loose the substance."[70] A greatly relieved President informed the Secretary of State that "the Land holders of Georgetown and Carrollsburg" agreed "That all the land from Rock creek along the river to the Eastern-branch and so upwards to or above the ferry including a breadth of about a mile and a half, the whole containing from three to five thousand acres is ceded to the public, on condition That, when the whole shall be surveyed and laid off as a city, (which Major L'Enfant is now directed to do) the present Proprietors shall retain every other lot—and, for such part of the land as may be taken for public use, for squares, walks, &ca—they shall be allowed at the rate of Twenty five pounds per acre,—No compensation is to be made for the ground that may be occupied as streets or alleys."[71] With this generous agreement, the small federal city that Washington and Jefferson had previously discussed would not be necessary. "The enlarged plan of this agreement having done away the necessity, and indeed postponed the propriety, of designating the particular spot, on which the public buildings should be placed, until an accurate survey and sub-division of the whole ground is made," Washington told Jefferson, "I have left out that paragraph of the proclamation."[72]

The President Gives Instructions

Before leaving Georgetown for his home and the beginning of his extensive tour of the Southern States, the President met with the Commissioners, Ellicott, and L'Enfant to give them final instructions "with respect to the mode of laying out the district—Surveying the grounds for the City and forming them into lots."[73] Washington again communicated with L'Enfant on April 4, sending him two plans for his *"private inspection."*[74] Both, he noted, "have been drawn by different persons, and under different circumstances."[75] One was Jefferson's "rough sketch" (Figure 9) drawn before the President's successful meeting with the proprietors. Washington carefully pointed out to L'Enfant that it "was done under an idea that *no* offer, worthy of consideration, would come from the Land holders in the vicinity of Carrollsburg (from the backwardness which appeared in them); and therefore, was accommodated to the grounds about George Town."[76] The second plan was simply described by Washington as having been "taken up upon a larger scale, without reference to any described spot.—"[77] Most likely, however, it was a plan sent to the President on December 5, 1790 by Joseph Clarke of Annapolis, Maryland.[78]

In the letter accompanying the two maps, Washington instructed L'Enfant to incorporate "as much ground (to be ceded by individuals) as there is any tolerable prospect of obtaining." This, he felt would insure that the plan would be "freed from those blotches [i.e., unplanned subdivisions], which otherwise might result from not comprehending *all* the lands that appear well adapted to the general design." The plan, Washington felt, should encompass those lands "betwee[n] Rock Creek, the Potowmac river and the Eastern branch, as far up the latter as the turn of the channel above Evans' point;—thence including the flat back of Jenkinss' height;—thence to the Road leading from George Town to Bladensburgh, as far Easterly alon[g] the same as to include the branch which runs across it, somewhere near the exterior of the George Town cession;—thence in a proper direction to Rock Creek at, or above the ford, according to the situation of the ground."[79] L'Enfant accepted without question the President's viewpoint and his plan was subsequently designed to encompass these geographical limits.

Jefferson Provides Some Plans and Some Advice

L'Enfant threw himself into the daunting task of designing a new capital city where only forests and plantations then stood. He requested the Secretary of State "as speedily as possible," to send him "The number and nature of the publick building[s]." In addition, he asked that plans be procured for him of several European cities, "such as for Example—as London—madry [i.e., Madrid]—paris—Amsterdam—naples—venice—genoa—florence together with particular maps of any such sea ports or dock yards and arsenals as you may know to be the most compleat in thier Improvement."[80] L'Enfant quickly explained to Jefferson that it was not his intention to imitate these plans, but rather to learn from them. He hoped that they "may serve to suggest a variety of new Ideas" and to assist him "to refine and Strengthen the [i.e., his] Jugement."[81]

Of the plans cited, Jefferson was able to send him his personal copies of Paris and Amsterdam. In addition, he supplied L'Enfant with Frankfurt am Main and Karlsruhe, Germany; Strasbourg, Orleans, Bordeaux, Lyons, Montpellier and Marseilles, France; and Turin and Milan, Italy, asking only that he "return them when no longer useful to you, leaving you absolutely free to keep them as long as useful."[82] Regarding public buildings, Jefferson suggested that since the President had obtained such favorable arrangements for obtaining the needed land, "I think very liberal reservations should be made for them, and if this be about the Tyber and on the back of the town it will be of no injury to the commerce of the place, which will undoubtedly establish itself on the deep waters towards the Eastern branch & mouth of Rock creek; the water about the mouth of the Tyber not being of any depth. Those connected with the government will prefer fixing themselves near the public grounds in the center, which will also be convenient to be resorted to as walks from the lower & upper town."[83]

Jefferson resisted the opportunity to express his opinions on how the new city should be laid out, noting only that he had communicated these ideas to the President before he left Philadelphia and that he was confident that "in explaining himself to you on the subject, he has interwoven with his own ideas, such of mine as he approved."[84]

Jefferson did offer L'Enfant his views on the appropriate style of architecture for the Capitol and the President's House. "Whenever it is proposed to prepare plans for the Capitol," he advised, "I should prefer the adoption of some one of the models of antiquity which have had the approbation of thousands of years; and for the President's house, I should prefer the celebrated fronts of Modern buildings which have already received the approbation of all good judges. Such are the Galerie du Louvre, the Gardes meubles, and two fronts of the Hotel de Salm."[85]

L'Enfant Meets Again with the President

During the months of April, May, and June 1791, L'Enfant worked intensively on the preparation of a written report and a preliminary plan of the capital city. Visitors to Georgetown such as the artist John Trumbull reported finding him hard at work "drawing his plan of the city of Washington."[86] Representative William Loughton Smith of South Carolina toured the site on April 22 in the company of L'Enfant. He noted in his journal that "The Major [i.e., L'Enfant] showed me all his plans and surveys, and so did Mr. Ellicott who is appointed to take the heights, distances, etc." Pleased with what he had seen, Smith wrote that he "returned to my tavern in the dusk of the evening well satisfied that the place selected unites more advantages for the place intended than any spot I have seen in America."[87]

Writing to James Madison, Commissioner Daniel Carroll noted that the Commissioners were scheduled to meet with the President on June 27. It was expected that at that time "Majr. L'Enfant will be ready agreeably to his instructions, with a description of the grounds within the City—it is probable some plans of the City and the public buildings may be then exhibited."[88]

Sometime between June 22 and 27 L'Enfant visited President Washington at Mount Vernon and presented him with a lengthy memoir accompanied by a preliminary draft of his plan of the city which he characterized as "an Incompleat drawing only correct as to the Situation and distances of objects."[89]

In executing his preliminary plan, L'Enfant explained to the President that after "having first determined some principal points to which I wished making the rest subordinate I next made the distribution regular with Streets at right angle *north-south* & *East-West* but afterwards I opened other[s] on various directions as avenues to & *from Every* principal place."[90] The diagonal avenues were introduced "principally to connect each part of the City . . . making the real distance less from place to place," thereby encouraging "rapide Stellement [i.e., settlement] over the whole so that the most remot[e] may become an adition to the principal."[91] L'Enfant also pointed out that several of the avenues were designed to join with roads coming into the city thus "rendering these Road[s] Shorter as is done with respect to the bladensburg & Eastern branche Road."[92] The avenues, L'Enfant noted, will provide the citizens with "a variety of pleasent ride[s]" and also "insure a rapide Inter course with all the part[s] of the City to which they will Serve as doses [i.e., does] the main vains in the animal body to diffuse life through smaller vessells in quickening the active motion of the heart."[93]

L'Enfant suggested to Washington that "a canal being easy to open from the Entrance of the eastern branch and to be lead [i.e., led] a cross the first Settlements and carried towards the mouth of the tiber were [i.e., where] it will again give an issue into the potowmack . . ., will undoubtedly facilitate a conveyance most advantageous to trading interest[s]."[94] The planner proposed to beautify the canal and the city by having Tiber Creek cascade forty feet down the west side of Jenkins' Hill, thereby producing "the most happy effect in rolling down to fill up the canall and discharge itself in the potowmack."[95] The entrance of the canal into the Potomac River, he recommended, should be restricted to 200 feet in width "to avoid its being drained at low water."[96] On the shore of the Potomac near the canal entrance at the point where the axes of the President's House and the

Capitol meet, L'Enfant proposed to "Erect A grand Equestrian figure" of George Washington which had been authorized by the Continental Congress as early as 1783.[97]

After carefully examining the terrain, L'Enfant concluded that he "could discover none so advantageous to Erect the Congressional building as is that on the west end of Jenkins heights which stand as a pedestal waiting for a monument."[98] For the "seat of the presidial [i.e., presidential] palace," L'Enfant suggested "that ridge which attracted your attention at the first inspection of the ground on the west side of the tiber Entrance." The city planner told Washington that the house will be visible from "10 or 12 miles down the potowmack front [i.e., from] the town and harbor of allexandria and Stand to the view of the whole City."[99]

"Fixed as Expressed on the map," L'Enfant believed that the distance separating the President's House from the Capitol "will not be to[o] great" because "a sort of decorum" will have to exist between the two branches of government. "To mak[e] how ever the distance less to other offices I placed the three grand departments of States [i.e., State, Treasury, and War] Contigous to the presidial [i.e., presidential] palace."[100] Connecting the Executive branch of government with the Legislative branch he suggested an avenue and a park and gardens containing a public walk "all long side of which may be placed play house—room of assembly—accademies and all such sort of places as may be attractive to the l[e]arned and afford diversion to the idle."[101]

Based on L'Enfant's report, it is clear that by June 22, 1791, the basic elements of his city plan had been formulated. All that was needed now was the President's approval to put this unique design for the capital city into motion.

L'Enfant's Preliminary Plan Is Displayed

On June 28, in the company of L'Enfant and Ellicott, the President rode over the area "to take a more perfect view of the ground, in order to decide finally on the spots on which to place the public buildings and to direct how a line which was to leave out a Spring (commonly known by the name of the Cool Spring) belonging to Majr. Stoddard should be run."[102] Satisfied with his inspection of the terrain, he called the local landholders together to inform them of the sites he had selected for public buildings. The President recorded in his dairy that at this meeting L'Enfant's preliminary plan was displayed "in order to convey to them general ideas of the City—but they were told that some deviation from it would take place—particularly in the diagonal streets or avenues, which would not be so numerous; and in the removal of the Presidents house more westerly for the advantage of higher ground—they were also told that a Town house, or exchange wd be placed on some convenient ground between the spots designed for the public buildgs. before mentioned.—and it was with much pleasure that a general approbation of the measure seemed to pervade the whole."[103]

During the next month and a half the site of the new town was a beehive of activity. Field surveys were intensified, trees were felled, and foundations for buildings begun. L'Enfant, having received Washington's general acceptance of his ideas for the city, was busy revising his plan to incorporate the changes recommended by the President and, as time permitted, working on his architectural drawings of the Capitol and the President's House.

L'Enfant's August Report

L'Enfant prepared a lengthy report for the President's consideration on August 19, in which he discussed various aspects of his plan, offered suggestions on the settlement of the city, and recommended the government obtain a substantial loan to permit the more rapid construction of the city and its public buildings. Accompanying his report was a "map of doted lines being sufficiently explanatory of the progress made in

the work [which] will I hope leave you satisfied how much more has been done than may have been expected from hands less desirous of meriting your applause."[104]

L'Enfant freely admitted that "this business has proved more tedious than at first considered owing to the multiplicity of operations Indispensable to determine the acute angles & intersect lines with exactness on points given at great distances."[105] Surveying difficulties had been further exacerbated by the great amount "of timber cut down in Every direction . . . which the proprietor[s] are avare [i.e., aware] to preserve [i.e., preserve for a profit] and unwilling to remove."[106]

The city planner also called the President's attention to "the frindly [i.e., friendly] assistance given me by Mr. Ellicotts" and asked if his planned trip to "the frontier of Georgi[a]" may be "differed [i.e., deferred] until the latter End of November next. his assistance till then being most indispensable to compleat the work begone [i.e., begun] as is necessary to have a number of lots for Houses measured and marked before the time when the first sale is Intended."[107]

Concerned about the progress of his field work, L'Enfant suggested that the first sale of lots in the new city announced for October 17 be delayed. L'Enfant pointed out that the proposed sale would be "so premature [that it] will not bring th[e] ten part of what it will at some more suitable season."[108] He further warned that only a few land speculators would profit by "a sale made previous [to] the general plan of distribution of the city is made publique and befor the circumstance of that sale taking place has had time to be know [i.e., known] through the whole continent."[109]

The President Reviews
L'Enfant's Plan and Report

Sometime between August 19 and 25, L'Enfant journeyed to Philadelphia and on or before August 26, he submitted to the President his written report accompanied by the "map of doted lines" and his presentation copy of the plan of the city. In the course of Washington's review of the materials several issues were raised that required immediate resolution, especially whether or not the first sale of lots should be delayed. This was the first of thirteen questions posed by Washington to Jefferson and the Commissioners to get their opinions. The questions are as follows:

[1.] Will circumstances render a postponement of the Sale of Lots in the Federal City advisable? If not
2. Where ought they to be made
3. Will it in that case, or even without it, be necessary or prudent to attempt to borrow money to carry on the difft. works in the City?

[4.] Whether ought the building of a bridge over the Eastern branch to be attempted—the Canal set about—and Mr. Peter's propo[si]tion with respect to wharves gone into *now*—or postponed until our funds are better ascertained and become productive?—
[5.] At what time can the several Proprietors claim, with propriety, payment for the public squares wch. is marked upon their respective tracts?—
[6.] Ought there to be any wood houses in the town?
7. What sort of Brick or Stone Houses should be built—& of wht. height—especially on the principal Streets or Avenues?
[8.] When ought the public buildings to be begun, & in what manner had the materials best be provided?—
[9.] How ought they to be promulgated, so as to draw plans from skilful architects? & what would be the best mode carrying on the Work?
[10.] Ought not Stoups & projections of every sort & kind into the Streets to be prohibited *absolutely*?
11. What compromise can be made with the Lot holders in Hamburgh & Carrollsburgh by which the plan of the Federal City may be preserved?
[12.] Ought not the several Land holders to be called upon to ascertain their respective boundaries previous to the Sale of Lots?
13. Would it not be advisable to have the Federal district as laid out (comprehending the plan of the Town), engraved in one piece?[110]

Jefferson and Madison Meet
with the Commissioners

Jefferson invited James Madison to his home on Friday, August 26, noting in the invitation that "the President has been here, & left L'Enfant's plan, with a wish that you & I would examine it together immediately, as to certain matters, & let him know the result."[111] Two days later, after discussions with Washington, Madison, and perhaps L'Enfant and others, the Secretary of State informed the Commissioners that "Major Lenfant . . . laid his plan of the Federal city before the President." After holding discussions with several persons on the subject, "it is the opinion of the President . . . that an immediate meeting of the Commissioners at George town is requisite, that certain measures may be decided on and put into a course of preparation for a commencement of sale on the 17th. of Octob. as advertised. as Mr. Madison & myself, who were present at the conferences, propose to pass through George town on our way to Virginia, the President supposes that our attendance at the meeting of the Commissioners might be of service to them, as we could communicate to them the sentiments developed at the conferences here & approved by the President."[112] It is not clear how much L'Enfant was involved in the discussions. The written record informs us only that he was invited to meet with the President on August 27 and to dine with Jefferson and Madison on September 1. The latter was arranged to inform L'Enfant about the upcoming September 8 meeting with the Commissioners and to brief him on the issues

that were to be decided or had been already decided by the President.[113]

L'Enfant Fails to Get His Plan Published

While in Philadelphia, L'Enfant took steps to have his plan of the city published. Earlier, Jefferson had told him that he had been approached "on the subject of engraving a Map of the Federal territory," but he had said that if such a map is contemplated either L'Enfant or Ellicott "would have the best right to it."[114] L'Enfant, therefore, contracted with Nareisse Pigalle, an obscure French engraver working in Philadelphia, to make the engraving. Into his hands, L'Enfant entrusted a reduced but incomplete copy of the plan which had been "drawn upon silk Paper" by his assistant Stephen Hallet.[115] Unfortunately, Pigalle first had difficulty in procuring the copperplate needed for the undertaking and then was unable to complete the engraving because of the lack of time before the first sale of lots was held and the failure of L'Enfant promptly to provide him with a complete copy of the plan.[116]

The sale of lots on October 17, therefore, was conducted before the published map became available. To compound the problem, L'Enfant prevented the display of his own copy of the "general plan at the spot were [i.e., where] the sale is made."[117] He was convinced that the lots would sell for less if the buyer was able to "compare the situation offered for sale with many other[s] more apparently advantageous."[118]

Despite his disappointment in the lack of a published map to advertise the new city, Washington wrote David Stuart that he could not "be of opinion the delays were occasioned by L'Enfant."[119] He was clearly disturbed, however, by L'Enfant's failure to display his general plan. Angrily, the President wrote that L'Enfant "conceives, or would have others believe, that the Sale was promoted by with-holding the general map, & thereby, the means of comparison; but I have caused it to be signified to him, that I am of a different opinion; & that it is much easier to impede, than to force a Sale, as none who knew what they were about would be induced to buy, to borrow an old adage 'A Pig in a Poke.' "[120]

The L'Enfant-Carroll Dispute

No sooner had this issue settled down when the President was faced with another crisis, this time involving a dispute between his planner and Daniel Carroll of Duddington, the largest landholder in the city.[121] The dispute began in August when L'Enfant ran the survey lines for the portion of New Jersey Avenue south of

Capitol Hill and discovered that Carroll's house, which was then under construction, protruded into the right-of-way by some seven feet. Not being able to reach a satisfactory agreement with L'Enfant, Carroll bypassed the Commissioners and brought the matter to the President's attention. Washington carefully reviewed the delicate situation hoping to avoid an embarrassing public airing of the grievance. In his response to Carroll he suggested "two alternatives: first, to arrest and pull down the building in its present State, and raise it to the same height next Spring—if it is your desire—agreeably to the regulations wch. have been established, without any expence to you—or, 2dly. to permit you to finish it at your own cost, and occupy it 6 years from the present date; at which period it *must* be removed with no other allowance from the Public than a valuation for the Walls in the present State of them."[122] On the same day (November 28), Washington sent L'Enfant a copy of his letter to Carroll, and in the covering letter cautioned him that "it will always be found sound policy to conciliate the good-will rather than provoke the enmity of any man, where it can be accomplished without much difficulty, inconvenience or loss.—Indeed the more harmoniously this, or any other business is conducted the faster it will progress, & the more satisfactory will it be."[123] Regrettably, the suggested solutions and the words of advice were received too late. L'Enfant, acting swiftly and on his own volition, had already pulled down the offending house. To further inflame the situation, L'Enfant and his assistants ignored orders from the Commissioners "to desist in pulling down Mr. Carroll's house in the City."[124]

Upon learning of L'Enfant's actions, Washington requested that Jefferson review the correspondence pertaining to Carroll's house and advise him on "how far he [i.e., L'Enfant] may be spoken to in decisive terms without loosing his services; which, in my opinion would be a serious misfortune.—At the same time *he must know*, there is a line beyond which he will not be suffered to go."[125]

As a result of this careful review, made not only by Jefferson but also by Madison, Washington sternly warned L'Enfant on December 2, that "In future I must strictly enjoin you to touch no man's property without his consent, or the previous order of the Commissioners.—I wish you to be employed in the arrangements of the Federal City: I still wish it: but only on condition that you can conduct yourself in subordination to the authority of the Commissioners . . . Your precipitate conduct will . . . give serious alarm, & produce disagreeable consequences.—Having the beauty, & harmony of your Plan only in view, you pursue it as if every person, and thing was *obliged* to yield to it; whereas the Commissioners

have many circumstances to attend to, some of which, perhaps, may be unknown to you; which evinces, in a strong point of view, the propriety, the necessity & even the safety of your acting by their directions.—"[126]

Finishing the Plan and Preparing It for Engraving

In his November 28th letter to L'Enfant, Washington again reminded his city planner of the urgency to get his map ready for publication before the second sale of lots in the spring so that "correct Engravings of the City could be had, and properly disseminated (*at least*) through out the United States before such sale."[127] To this end, L'Enfant arranged with Benjamin Ellicott to "delinate on paper all the work which had been done in the city, which being accurately measured, and permanently laid down on the Ground."[128]

Preserved in the Library of Congress is an anonymous manuscript map showing the status of surveys in the new city at a very early date (Figure 10). Although lacking a title and other

Figure 10. Map showing the status of surveys in Washington, D.C., probably drawn in December 1791 by Benjamin Ellicott. *Geography and Map Division, LC.*

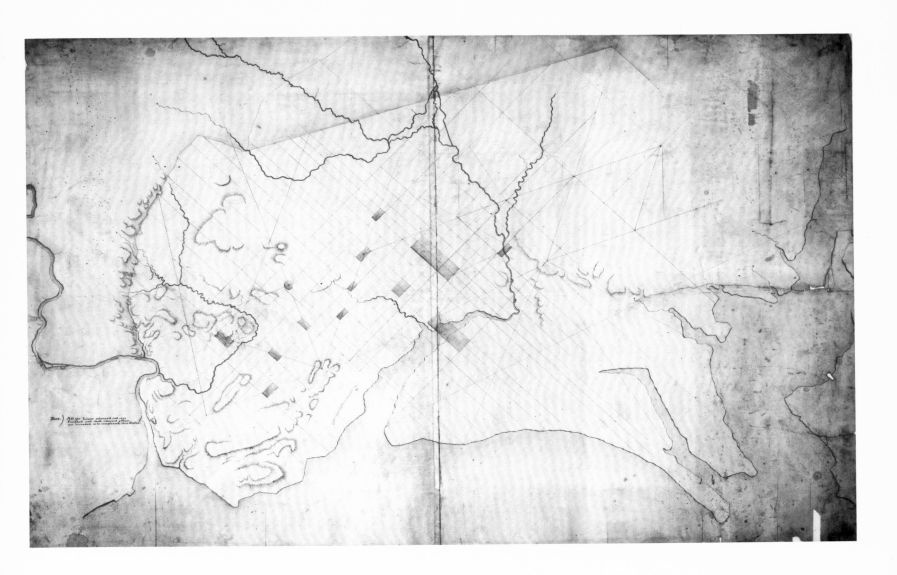

Note.) All the lines coloured red are finished and their coloured faces are intended to be emphasized thus shaded.

35

identifying information, a single explanatory note states that "All the Lines coloured red, are finished and those coloured yellow are intended to be compleated this Season." Measuring 68 × 106 cm., it is drawn on two sheets of eighteenth-century paper that have been pasted together. The right sheet contains the watermark of Thomas Budgen, the same English mill that manufactured the paper used by L'Enfant for the plan presented to President Washington in August, and the left sheet includes the watermark of the rival paper mill of James Whatman. Based on its content, it is likely that this is the map that L'Enfant requested Benjamin Ellicott to make in December 1791, to show the current status of their field work. It more closely agrees with the layout of the city as proposed in the published version of the L'Enfant plan prepared by the Ellicott brothers in February 1792. Massachusetts Avenue, for example, is shown as a straight line and not with a bend in it as it initially appeared in the August plan. It was L'Enfant's intention "to make the basis of the drawing of the remainder from the original plan, and upon a reduced Scale for Engraving."[129] For reasons that are obscure, L'Enfant was unable to obtain the drawing from Ellicott before departing for Philadelphia late in December 1791. It simply may not have been finished in time for his departure. "Not having had it in my possession," L'Enfant wrote,

"prevented me immediately on my arrival here, to have the reduced drawing began according to my Intention & promise to the president."[130] Unable to engage a good draughtsman in Philadelphia, L'Enfant again arranged with Benjamin Ellicott to produce an updated but reduced version of his plan that would be suitable for engraving. Although Ellicott was "not professional in drawing," L'Enfant believed that he was "the most proper person to prepar the work in that part more Especially which himself and Mr. Roberdeau had with accuracy laid down upon the ground."[131] To aid Ellicott in his work, L'Enfant supplied him with Hallet's incomplete "sketch" which had been prepared six months earlier for the Philadelphia engraver Pigalle. At L'Enfant's request, Tobias Lear, the President's secretary, had retrieved the drawing from Hallet.[132]

Andrew Ellicott Takes Over

L'Enfant reported that he "daily attended the progress of the business in all its stages" until he was told that Jefferson had instructed Andrew Ellicott to finish the drawing for the engraver.[133] L'Enfant then removed himself from the day-to-day supervision of the plan, obviously upset by this turn of events but confident that he would be responsible for its final editing and verification.

Suspecting that something was amiss, however, L'Enfant visited Ellicott's house and to his surprise found the draft "in the State in which it now is most unmercifully spoiled and altered from the original plan."[134]

On February 15, the President wrote to the Secretary of State that he did not wish to express an opinion "on the alterations proposed for the engraved plan" until he had an opportunity to converse with Jefferson "on several matters which relate to this business."[135] Washington received the finished plan from Andrew Ellicott on Monday, February 20, 1792.[136]

Two days later, the President had the plan on his mind and was obviously upset by the necessity of bypassing L'Enfant to obtain a finished drawing for the engraver. "The Plan I think, ought to appear as the Work of L'Enfant," wrote Washington. "The one prepared for engraving not doing so, is, I presume, one cause of his dissatisfaction."[137] Washington went on to suggest that if L'Enfant "consents to act upon the conditions proposed," then it might be wise to employ him to "point out any radical defects, or others to amend."[138] These suggestions were not implemented; the manuscript was not examined by L'Enfant before being sent to the engraver; and the map was published without any attribution to him. Why the President's suggestions, especially identifying L'Enfant as

the creator of the plan, were not carried out, remains a mystery. The failure to include L'Enfant's name on the published maps denied him the honor he deserved and caused bitterness and rancor between the planner and the Commissioners and government for years to come. Nearly six years later, for example, when the matter of differences between the L'Enfant and Ellicott versions of the plan was raised by proprietor Samuel Davidson, Commissioner Thomas Johnson is quoted as saying "with some degree of warmth—'God damn it, are we never to get clear of L'Enfant.' "[139]

It is not clear what Andrew Ellicott contributed to the form of the plan itself, but because of the brief time in which he was directly involved, it may have been relatively little. Ellicott had been employed to conduct the necessary surveys and not to plan the city. During 1791 his relationship with L'Enfant had remained cordial and he provided geodetic control and surveying assistance as needed. His chief responsibility, however, was to survey and mark the boundary of the ten-mile-square Federal Territory, an undertaking not completed until December 1792.[140] In addition, in November and December 1791, he was engaged in surveying squares along Pennsylvania Avenue.[141]

Andrew Ellicott's direct association with the plan began when he arrived in Philadelphia and "found that no preparation was made for an engraving of the plan of the City of Washington."[142] He informed the President and the Secretary of State of the situation and "was directed to furnish one for an engraver which with the aid of my Brother was compleated last Monday and handed to the President."[143] Ellicott informed the Commissioners that he had "engaged two good artists (both Americans,) to execute the engraving."[144] The reference to "both Americans" was obviously meant as a comparison to L'Enfant's failed attempt to produce a map for the first sale of lots after having hired an engraver of French origin.[145] Ellicott also reported to the Commissioners that they had met serious difficulty in compiling the map because "Major L'Enfant refused us the use of the *Original*! What his motives were, God knows."[146] This conflicts with L'Enfant's statement that he was confident that the plan "would not be completely finished without recourse to the large map in my possession. I conceived it would be but proper to wait until I was called upon by him to review and correct the whole."[147]

Ellicott's Sources

Although the Ellicott brothers did not use L'Enfant's "large map" for whatever reason, they did have Benjamin's up-to-date drawing showing the status of field work (Figure 10), probably field surveys of portions of the city, including Andrew's recent surveys of the squares along Pennsylvania Avenue, and Hallet's partially completed drawing of the L'Enfant plan. Certainly before their drawing was finished, Washington and Jefferson shared with them the plan that L'Enfant had presented to the President in August 1791. It is from this plan, in fact, that most of the textual information was taken, although the map itself was considerably altered. Confirmation that the earlier L'Enfant plan was used is found in Washington's letter to the Commissioners in which he transferred the plan to their keeping: "This plan you shall receive by the first safe hand who may be going to the Federal City—By it you may discover (tho' almost obliterated) the directions given to the Engraver, by Mr. Jefferson, with a pencil, what parts to omit."[148]

Jefferson Edits L'Enfant's Plan

Careful examination of the L'Enfant plan now preserved in the Library of Congress reveals the faint pencil corrections referred to by the President. The corrections, apparently in Jefferson's handwriting, are editorial rather than substantive, giving instructions regarding what words and phrases to delete, to substitute, and to add. With two exceptions, the corrections were incorporated into the finished plan submitted by Andrew Ellicott to the President for publication.[149]

Although many of the pencil notations are illegible today, as they were in 1796 when Washington referred the manuscript plan to the Commissioners, it is possible to decipher some with the naked eye. For example, in every instance where L'Enfant had written "Congress House," both on the map as well as in the notes, these words have been changed to read "Capitol," the term preferred by Jefferson. The Ellicott version exclusively uses the word "Capitol." A complete list of the visible editorial changes made by Jefferson appears in the accompanying table (Figure 11).

The Published Plans

The finished manuscript was given to Thackara and Vallance of Philadelphia (Ellicott's "Americans") to engrave. Before beginning their work on the large engraving, the partners prepared a reduced version for publication as the frontispiece in the March 1792 issue of *The Universal Asylum, and Columbia Magazine* (Figure 12). This small rendering became the first depiction of the plan of the capital city to receive wide circulation. Meanwhile, when Washington learned that it would take the partners at least eight weeks to engrave the map, he asked Jefferson, "Is not this misteriously strange!"[150] The President, ever suspicious of the delaying tactics employed by Philadelphians anxious to see the city on the Potomac fail, thought it likely that "they may keep it eight months."[151] With this preying on his mind he suggested to the Secretary of State that a copy of the map be secretly prepared and sent to an engraver in another city, perhaps Boston or London.[152] Because of his concern, arrangements were made through Samuel Blodget, Jr. for a second engraving to be made by Samuel Hill of Boston.

It was the Hill engraving that was first to be completed, arriving in Philadelphia on July 20, where arrangements were made for Mr. Scott to print 4000 copies. To accomplish this, the printer made approximately one-hundred impressions a day until the undertaking was completed. Prints of the Hill engraving were in circulation at the second sale of lots held in the City of Washington on October 8, 1792[153] (Figure 13).

Although copies of the Thackara and Vallance engraving were available too late for use during the second public sale of lots, it was considered far more elegant in appearance and was accepted quickly as the "official" published version of the plan (Figure 14). Not only was the Philadelphia plate better engraved, it had been

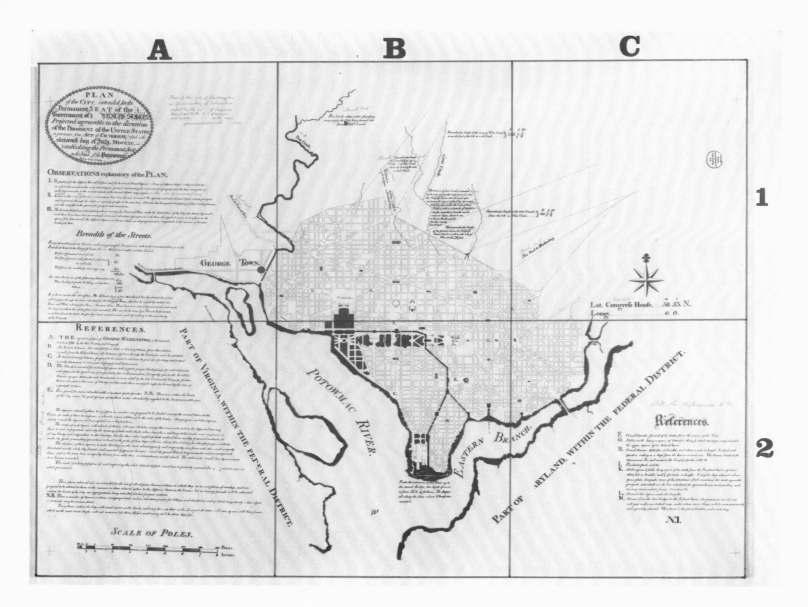

A **B** **C**

1

2

40

Figure 11.

TABLE AND DIAGRAM OF EDITORIAL CHANGES MADE BY THOMAS JEFFERSON TO THE L'ENFANT PLAN

Grid Reference	L'Enfant Plan	Deletions and Additions (Additions are Underlined)	Grid Reference	L'Enfant Plan	Deletions and Additions (Additions are Underlined)
A–1	Plan of the City, intended for the Permanent Seat of the Government of t[he] United States. Projected agreeable to the direction of the President of the United States, in pursuance of an Act of Congress, passed on the sixteenth day of July, MDCCXC, —"establishing the Permanent Seat on the bank of the Potowmac." By Peter Charles L'Enfant.— Observations explanatory of the Plan. Line 1: The positions for the different Grand Edifices, and for the several Grand Squares or Areas, of different shapes as they are laid dow[n] Line 3: such improvements as the various intents of the several objects may require. Line 9: spaces "first determined," the different Squares or Areas, which	[To right of L'Enfant's title:] Plan of the city of Washington in the territory of Columbia ceded by the Sta[tes] of Virginia and Mariland to the U.S. of America and by them [established] as the Seat [of their] government after the [year] 1800 The positions for the different Edifices, and for the several Squares or Areas of different shapes as they are laid dow[n] such improvements as either use or ornament may [here]after [call] for spaces "first determined," the different Squares or Areas,		are all proportional in magnitude to the number of Avenues Line 10: leading to them. Breadth of the Streets Line 1: Every grand transverse Avenue, and every principal divergent one, such as the communication from the Line 2: President's house to the Congress house, &c: is 160 feet in breadth, and thus divided, Line 10: In order to execute the above plan, Mr. Ellicott drew a true meridional line by celestial observation Line 11: which passes through the Area intended for the Congress house; this line he crossed by another due [To right of] Observations explanatory of the Plan.	[lined out] Every grand transverse Avenue, and every principal divergent one, from the is 160 feet in breadth, and thus divided, In order to execute this plan, Mr. Ellicott drew a true meridional line by celestial observation which passes through the Area intended for the Capitol; this line he crossed by another due

Figure 11.—Cont.

TABLE AND DIAGRAM OF EDITORIAL CHANGES MADE BY THOMAS JEFFERSON TO THE L'ENFANT PLAN

Grid Reference	L'Enfant Plan	Deletions and Additions (Additions are Underlined)	Grid Reference	L'Enfant Plan	Deletions and Additions (Additions are Underlined)
	Road to Frederick Town.	Road from Frederick Town. Struck Out [written above line.]		watering that part of the City, its overplus will fall from under the base of that	City, may be destined to other useful purposes.
A–2	References	[Diagonal line marked through References] [Left margin, written vertically:] All to be struck out		Edifice, and in a cascade of 20 feet in height, and 50 in breadth into the reservoir below; thence to run in three fills through the garden into the grand Canal.	[Diagonal line marked through a remainder of note]
B–1	Pine Creek.	Rock Creek.			
	Pine Creek whose water, if necessary, may supply the City, being turned into Jame[s] White's branch.	Struck Out [Diagonal line marked through note]		The perpendicular height of the ground where the Congress house stands, is above the tide of Tiber Creek, 78 feet.	The perpendicular height of the ground where the Capitol stands is above the tide of Tiber Creek, 78 feet.
	Perpendicular height of J[a]mes Whites spring, being p[ar]t of Tiber Creek, above the level of the tide in said Creek.	Struck Out [Diagonal line marked through note]		[Unnamed street on plan; K Street today]	K [Added to plan at junction of 17th and K streets, N.W.]
	This branch, an[d that of] the Tiber, [is in]-tended to be conveyed [to th]e President's house.	This branch, an[d that of] the Tiber, may be conveyed [to th]e President's house.	B–2	["Grand Avenue" running the length of the Mall. Labelled "H" in two places.]	Avenue a mile long and 400 feet wide
	The water of this Creek is intended to be conveyed on the high ground, where the Congress house stands, and after	The water of this Creek may be conveyed on the high ground, where the Capitol stands, and after watering that part of the		Potowmac River. Congress house.	[X marked through w in "Potowmac."] Capitol

Figure 11.—Cont.

TABLE AND DIAGRAM OF EDITORIAL CHANGES
MADE BY THOMAS JEFFERSON TO
THE L'ENFANT PLAN

Grid Reference	L'Enfant Plan	Deletions and Additions (Additions are Underlined)
C–1	Lat. Congress House, ...38°53'. N.	Lat. <u>Capitol</u>, ...38°53'N.
	<u>New Road to Bladens-burg</u>	Struck Out
C–2	References.	[Diagonal line marked through References.] <u>All the References to be</u> [struck out.]

produced on a larger sheet of copper measuring 52¾ by 71½ cm. compared to the Boston plate which measured 42 by 51½ cm.[154] Perhaps most importantly, however, it included the depths of water in the shipping channel and along the shore lines of the Potomac River and the Eastern Branch, information viewed as especially important by Washington, Jefferson, and other boosters for attracting merchant investors to the new city. The hydrographic data had been received too late for inclusion in the Boston plate.

With the exception of water depths and the addition of ten more squares on the Thackara and Vallance engraving, the two printed maps contain the same information.[155] Both maps incorporate the decisions reached by the Commissioners in conference with Jefferson and Madison on September 8, 1791. At this meeting it was decided on a new name for the city, a title for the planned map, and a logical method for identifying streets. In a letter mailed the next day, the Commissioners told L'Enfant, "We have agreed that the federal District shall be called 'The Territory of Columbia' and the federal City 'The City of Washington', the title of the map will therefore be 'A Map of the City of Washington in the Territory of Columbia.' We have also agreed the Streets be named alphabetically one way and numerically the other, the former divided into north and south Letters, the latter into east and west numbers from the Capitol."[156] It was probably Jefferson who suggested the use of letters and numbers for the streets. While serving as governor of Virginia in 1780, he was a member of the Board of Directors appointed by the General Assembly that recommended the same system of nomenclature for the city of Richmond.[157]

In addition to the decisions reached on September 8, the two published plans indicate the identifying numbers given for each square. The Hill engraving depicts 1136 numbered squares and the Thackara and Vallance engraving 1146. The avenues are named for the fifteen states

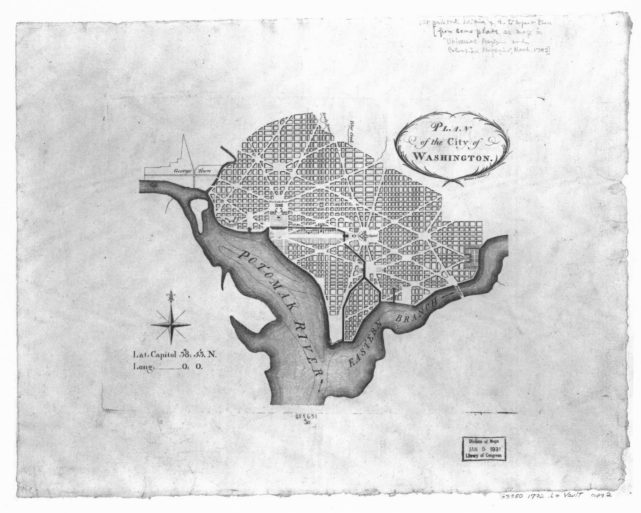

Figure 12. The first printed image of L'Enfant's plan appeared as the frontispiece in the March 1792 issue of *The Universal Asylum, and Columbia Magazine. Geography and Map Division, LC.*

44

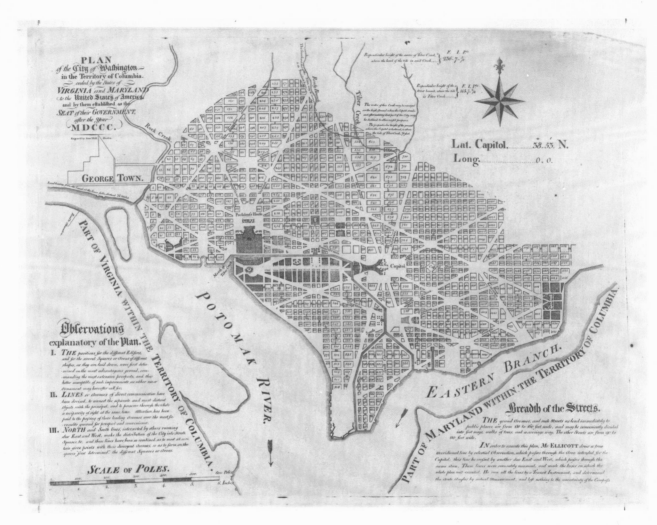

Figure 13. The L'Enfant plan of Washington as drawn by Andrew Ellicott and engraved by Samuel Hill of Boston in 1792. *Geography and Map Division, LC.*

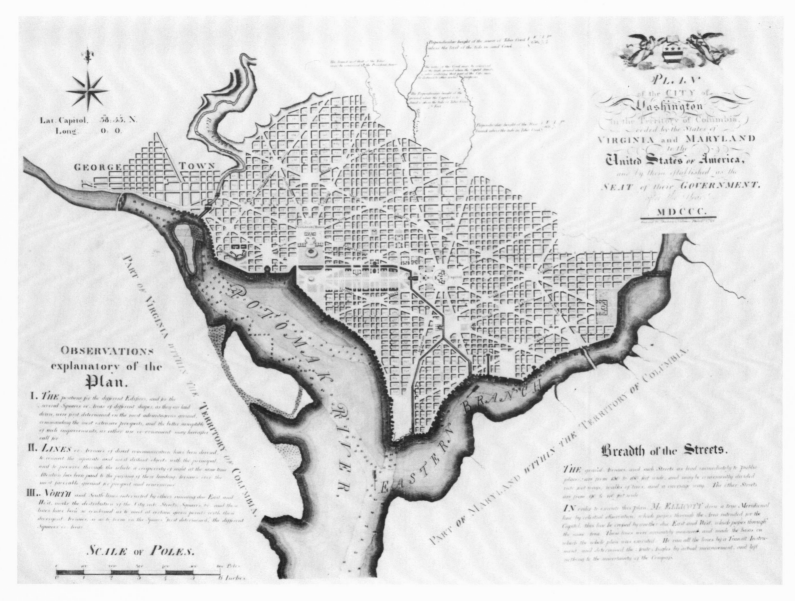

which then made up the Union. When the names were applied to the avenues and by whom is not certain. As late as December 10, 1791, Andrew Ellicott was still referring to Pennsylvania Avenue as "the Diagonal between George Town, and the Presidents House."[158] L'Enfant scholar Pamela Scott believes that L'Enfant was responsible for naming the avenues and has recently pointed out the geographical and political significance of their arrangement. In a presentation given at the National Gallery of Art on October 30, 1987, she noted that "The northeastern states were clustered in the northern segment of the city, the southern in the southeastern quadrant, and the mid-Atlantic states in the center, reflecting not only the country's geography, but also its regional, political, and social alignments."[159]

Both engravings of the Ellicott version of the L'Enfant plan also indicate fortifications at the point of land formed by the joining of the Eastern Branch with the Potomac and on the high land west of 23rd Street; two bridges crossing the Eastern Branch and one across the Potomac at Georgetown; the proposed canal system using the waters of Tiber Creek and St. James Creek; a tree-lined "Grand Avenue" running the length of the Mall; and finally, ground plans for seven major buildings, including the Capitol, the President's House, and a large, unidentified structure at the eastern juncture of Massachusetts and Georgia Avenues (Potomac Avenue today). A 1793 broadside states that the last was intended to be "a Marine Hospital."[160] The plans almost certainly are those of L'Enfant. He had been given instructions not only to prepare a ground plan for the new city but also to prepare designs for the public buildings. By the winter of 1791–1792, L'Enfant's building plans were well-advanced. Washington told Jefferson on February 22, that "The Plans of the buildings ought to come forward immediately for consideration.—I think Mr. Walker said yesterday he (L'Enfant) had been shewing the different views of them to Mr. Trumbul [i.e., John Trumbull]."[161] Further evidence that no other building plans were available during the winter months of 1791–1792 is found in the President's last communication with L'Enfant. "Five months," the disappointed President wrote, "have elapsed and are lost by the compliment which was intended to be paid you, in depending alone upon your plans for the public buildings, instead of advertising a premium to the person who should present the best (which would equally have included yourself)."[162]

Figure 14. The L'Enfant plan of Washington as drawn by Andrew Ellicott and engraved by Thackara and Vallance of Philadelphia in 1792. *Geography and Map Division, LC.*

L'Enfant's Removal

L'Enfant's removal from direct supervision of the plan was due to his apparent procrastination in finishing it promptly for publication. It seems unlikely, however, that he purposely delayed the completion of the plan, but rather was struggling to complete the countless details that go into a plan of a capital city encompassing more than 6000 acres. On January 17, 1792, at the same time he was supervising the drawing of his plan for publication, L'Enfant sent the President a detailed seventeen-point "estimate of the Labor & expences necessary to be employed in the federal city" in the ensuing season—hardly the kind of report to be expected from a man whom Andrew Ellicott was to describe a month later as having "both a lively fancy and decision [i.e., determination]; but unfortunately no system, which renders the other qualifications much less valuable, and in some cases useless."[163]

To expect one man in less than one year to create a plan for a new capital city; to supervise the laying out of the streets, avenues, and public lands; to prepare plans for public buildings; and to prepare a final drawing of the city plan for publication was unreasonable. Because a public works project of this scope had never been attempted before, there is little wonder that this creative genius' actions and intentions were misunderstood by the Commissioners, Jefferson, Andrew Ellicott, boosters of the city, and even the President, his chief supporter and himself a former land surveyor. The President, of course, viewed the wide circulation of a published map as a key element in enticing the public to buy lots in the new city. It was through the sale of property that he hoped to raise sufficient funds to advance the laying out of streets and squares and the construction of the public buildings that would be needed to accommodate the government when it moved from Philadelphia to Washington in 1800.

The President, therefore, was obviously alarmed when Andrew Ellicott informed him that on his arrival in Philadelphia he had "found that no preparation was made for an engraving of the plan of the City of Washington."[164] It was then, as we have seen, that Ellicott was requested to assume responsibility for finishing the reduced drawing and to make arrangements with an engraver to prepare the printing plate.

Despite L'Enfant's failure to hasten the completion of his map and his inability to work with the Commissioners or submit to their authority, the patient Washington was anxious to avoid firing his brilliant city planner, of whom he had earlier said, "for such employment as he is now engaged in;, for projecting public works—& carrying them into effect he was better qualified than any one who had come within my knowledge in this Country or indeed in any other the probability of obtaining whom could be counted upon."[165] On February 22, therefore, the Secretary of State wrote to L'Enfant that he was "charged by the President to say that your continuance would be desireable to him; & at the same time to add that the law requires it should be in subordination to the Commissioners."[166]

L'Enfant Refuses to Compromise

This L'Enfant could not accept. He answered that "If therefore the Law absolutely requires without any equivocation that my continuance shall depend upon an appointment from the Commissioners—I cannot, nor would I upon any Consideration submit myself to it."[167] To this Jefferson responded, "I am instructed by the President to inform you that notwithstanding the desire he has entertained to preserve your agency in the business, the condition upon which it is to be done is inadmissable, & your services must be at an end."[168]

The President's disappointment and frustration, as well as his resignation to the situation as it then stood is aptly summed up in his last letter to L'Enfant, written the day after his dismissal. Washington wrote, in part:

Your final resolution being taken, I shall delay no longer to give my ideas to the Commissioners for carrying into effect the Plan for the federal City.

The continuance of your services (as I have often assured you) would have been pleasing to me, could they have been retained on terms compatible with the law. Every mode has been tried to accommodate your wishes on this principle, except changing the Commissioners . . . . —To change the commissioners cannot be done on ground of propriety, justice or Policy.

Many weeks have been lost since you came to Philadelphia in obtaining a plan for engraving, notwithstanding the earnestness with which I requested it might be prepared on your first arrival.—further delay in this business is inadmissable.[169]

Thus was L'Enfant's role in the design of the capital for the new nation unhappily concluded.

L'Enfant's Later Years

Personal and financial success continued to elude L'Enfant in the years following his dismissal. The French Revolution had cost him his estate in France and his employment as a city planner, architect, and engineer failed to provide him with an adequate income. In 1800, L'Enfant sought payment from the City Commissioners and Congress for his services in creating the plan of the Nation's Capital. Washington journalist Benjamin Perley Poore wrote that "The Major then became an unsuccessful petitioner before Congress for a redress of his real and fancied wrongs, and he was to be seen almost every day slowly pacing the rotunda of the Capitol. . .. Under his arm he generally carried a roll of papers relating to his claim upon the Government, and in his right hand he swung a formidable hickory cane with a large silver head."[170] Although L'Enfant received some compensation from Congress, it was much less than he thought he deserved, and it was quickly exhausted to pay his debts.

Virtually penniless, L'Enfant spent the final decade of his life first as a dependent of Thomas A. Digges at Warburton Manor, Maryland, and then of William Dudley Digges at Green Hill, Maryland. "The old major," Thomas Digges wrote to Secretary of State James Monroe in 1816, "is still an inmate with me—quiet, harmless, & unoffending as usual—I fear from symptoms of broken shoes, rent pantaloons, out at elboes, & oder that he is not well off."[171] The "old major" died at Green Hill on June 14, 1825, ignored by many of his contemporaries, and his plan widely ridiculed as impractical and pretentious. Traveler John Melish astutely observed, however, that Pierre Charles L'Enfant had created "A Most elegant plan, and a very animated description. It only wants 40,000 elegant buildings, and a corresponding population, to constitute the American capital one of the handsomest cities in the world! However, it is to be recollected that every thing must have a beginning, and the time was when London was *not*."[172]

The August Plan

The plan that L'Enfant presented to the President on or before August 26, 1791, is believed to be the manuscript preserved in the Library of Congress. It is entitled "Plan of the City, intended for the Permanent Seat of the Government of t[he] United States. Projected agreeable to the direction of the President of the United States, in pursuance of an Act of Congress passed the sixteenth day of July, MDCCXC, 'establishing the Permanent Seat on the bank of the Potomac.' By Peter Charles L'Enfant." It is drawn on two pieces of laid paper joined at the center to form a writing surface measuring 73 by 103 cm.

Both sheets of paper bear the same watermark, a shield topped by a crown (Figure 15). On the shield is a fleur-de-lis with the initials TB on the petal. Below the shield appear the initials GR, signifying George Rex. This is the watermark used by the English papermaker Thomas Budgen. It is estimated that this paper was manufactured between 1779 and 1785.[173]

Although undated, the title of the manuscript plan and the absence of street numbers and letters are evidence that it was completed before the Commissioners, in conference with Jefferson and Madison on September 8, 1791, decided to name the city after George Washington and to identify the streets by numbers and letters of the alphabet.[174]

The surviving manuscript plan is not merely a tracing or a presentation copy, but gives every indication of being L'Enfant's original working draft that had been in a state of transition up to its delivery to the President in August 1791. There are numerous erasures and corrections, as well as pinholes that suggest they were made by compass and dividers in laying out the location of streets and avenues.[175] The pattern of streets and avenues is drawn in pencil, whereas the map title, notes, shore lines, and other details are added in ink. The use of pencil for the streets and avenues further suggests that this originally may have been a working draft.

Certainly by August 1791 the surviving working drawing had outlived its usefulness as L'Enfant had constructed another copy, apparently on an enlarged scale, to serve as his master map. Although there are references to his "original," "large," or "general" plan in textual records, this later map has not survived.[176]

There also is some evidence that without

Figure 15. One of the two identical watermarks from the paper on which the L'Enfant plan is drawn. It is the watermark used by the English papermaker Thomas Budgen for paper manufactured from about 1779 until 1785. The photograph was made in the Library's Conservation Office by using beta radiography.

L'Enfant's permission copies were made of his August plan, or even perhaps from his "large" plan. L'Enfant is quoted as saying that the August plan was "lodged in the best place of safety, into the hands of the President . . . . But although thus protected a number of my drawing copies had been made therefrom without my knowledge, such as were seen in both houses of Congress hanging on the Walls in December '91."[177] Mrs. Ann Brodeau wrote on December 22, 1791, to her son-in-law, William Thornton, the subsequent designer of the Capitol, "that there is a most elegant plan laid down for the Federal City. Mr. Cox is employed to take & embelish a copy of it for which he is to receive ten guineas from a gentleman of New York, I asked him for a rough sketch of it for you which he has promised me on a small scale taken from the Camera Obscura the one he is going to copy is laid down on four sheets of the largest Folio paper."[178] Mrs. Brodeau's reference to a map "on four sheets of the largest folio paper" would seem to indicate that this was an enlarged copy of the August plan or, possibly, L'Enfant's "large" plan itself, as the August plan is drawn on two sheets of folio paper, not four.

Before venturing to Philadelphia in August to discuss his proposals for the new city with the President, L'Enfant probably added a title to his old working copy, as well as extensive notes describing the salient elements of his "grand plan." He labeled the text "Observations explanatory of the Plan," "Breadth of the Streets," and "References." A handwritten draft for some of the notes is extant.[179] The six surviving pages, the first four in the hand of Andrew Ellicott and the final two in L'Enfant's hand, follow closely the text that was carefully lettered on the plan, but with two notable exceptions. The draft refers to "the Presidents Palace." This was wisely modified on the plan (line 2 of "Breadth of the Streets") to the more egalitarian "President's house." The draft also cites the "Heroick or Equestrian figure of George Washington." This was changed on the plan to "THE equestrian figure of George Washington" (line one of the "References"), with the space that "Heroick or" would have occupied filled by the capitalized letters of "THE."

In developing the framework for the plan, that is the streets and avenues, L'Enfant first selected "the most advantageous ground commanding the most extensive prospects" for placing the "different Grand Edifices, and for the several Grand Squares or Areas of different shapes." Crisscrossing the city, but focusing on several nodes, such as the sites for the "President's house" and the "Congress house," are avenues 160 feet wide "devised, to connect the separate and most distant objects with the principal, and to preserve through the whole a reciprocity of sight at the same time." Each avenue was to consist of "10 feet of pavement on each side," "30 feet of gravel Walk planted with trees on each side," and "80 feet in the middle for Carriage way." Streets of 90, 110, and 130 feet in width were to be laid out on "North and South lines, intersected by others running due East and West," creating the familiar rectangular or gridiron pattern found in most American cities.

At the center of his plan L'Enfant placed the "Congress house" on Jenkins' Hill (called "Heights" by L'Enfant), the site he had earlier noted "stand as a pedestal waiting for a monument," and to the west, on a low ridge with a view looking down the Potomac River, he placed the "President's house."[180]

Connecting the two dominant government buildings are a Mall laid out on an east-west axis and the "President's park" ("I" on the plan) and an adjoining "Well improved field" ("K" in the "References" but inadvertently left off the plan) on a north-south axis, creating a large, hatchet-shaped open space in the center of the city. Running the length of the Mall is a "Grand Avenue, 400 feet in breath, and about a mile in length, bordered with gardens, ending in a slope from the houses on each side" ("H" on the plan).

Lots along the Mall, L'Enfant suggested, are "some of the situations which command the most agreeable prospects, and which are the best calculated for spacious houses and gardens, such as may accommodate foreign ministers, &c." At the point of intersection of the axes he proposed placing "The equestrian figure of George Washington, a Monument voted in 1783, by the late Continental Congress" ("A" on the plan), a site near that occupied today by the obelisk of the Washington Monument.

L'Enfant's placement of the Capitol to the east and the President's House to the west connected by a promenade was first suggested by Jefferson in his sketch for the proposed city made in March 1791 (Figure 9). The idea of the Mall with its flanking buildings, however, may have been suggested by Jules Hardouin Mansart's plan of the royal chateau of Marly. In his study of the White House, William Seale has written that "this chateau was neglected during most of the 18th century, but its return to royal favor in the 1770s brought it back into the public eye while L'Enfant was a student in art school. There were remarkable similarities between L'Enfant's Mall, with its flanking buildings forming a vista to the Capitol, and the way the secondary buildings at Marly were organized along a central mall that stretched before the small palace. As in

Washington, the mall at Marly was open to the river and to distant hills. In the forests beyond the central mall of the palace of Marly numerous long diagonal streets intersected at circles, very much as do the streets in the city of Washington."[181] (Figure 16)

Another significant design feature was the introduction of a canal to replace the sluggish tidewater courses of St. James Creek and the lower Tiber Creek. The west side of the Capitol grounds features a "Grand Cascade formed of the Water from the sources of the Tiber" falling into the canal basin at the foot of Jenkins' Hill ("F" on the plan).

L'Enfant imagined a great commercial district on the eastern side of the Capitol and along the "Avenue from the two bridges to the Federal house, the pavement on each side will pass under an Arched way, under whose cover, shops will be most conveniently and agreeably situated" ("L" and "M" on the plan) (Figure 17). This avenue (now East Capitol Street) leads to "An historic Column—Also intended for a Mile or itinerary Column, from whose station, (a mile from the Federal house) all distances of places through the Continent, are to be calculated" (B on the plan). East Capitol Street did not become the commercial center that L'Enfant imagined, but rather a principal street in a large middle class residential neighborhood. The site selected

by L'Enfant for the itinerary column is now Lincoln Park containing the Emancipation Monument erected in 1876. The column was never erected on this site.

At the foot of what was to be 8th Street, S.W. on the shore of the Potomac River, L'Enfant proposed erecting "A Naval itinerary Column . . . to celebrate the first rise of a Navy, and to stand a ready monument to consecrate it progress and atchievments [sic]" (C on the plan).

Also on 8th Street, at the site now occupied by the National Museum of American Art and the National Portrait Gallery in the old Patent Office Building designed by William P. Elliot, L'Enfant suggested the erection of a nondenominational church "for national purposes, such as public prayer, thanksgivings, funeral Orations, &c. . . . It will be likewise a proper shelter for such monuments as were voted by the late Continental Congress, for those heroes who fell in the cause of liberty, and for such others as may hereafter be decreed by the voice of a grateful Nation" ("D" on the plan) (Figure 18).

Figure 16. Jules Hardouin Mansart's plan of the royal chateau of Marly may have given L'Enfant the idea of the Mall with its flanking buildings. This illustration entitled "Veue du Chateau et Parc de Marli" is from Gilles de Mortain's *Les Plans, Profils, et Elevations, des Ville et Chateau de Versailles* . . . (Paris, De Mortain, [1716]), plate 50. *Rare Book and Special Collections Division, LC.*

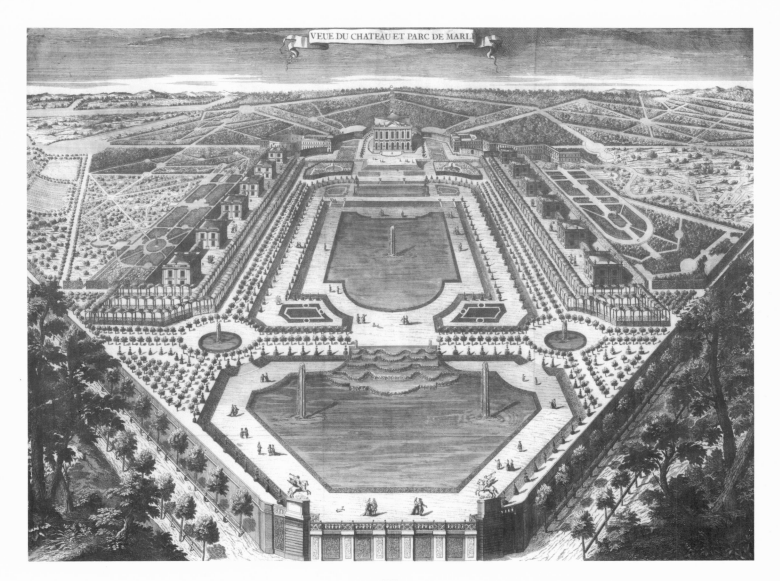

VEUE DU CHATEAU ET PARC DE MARLI

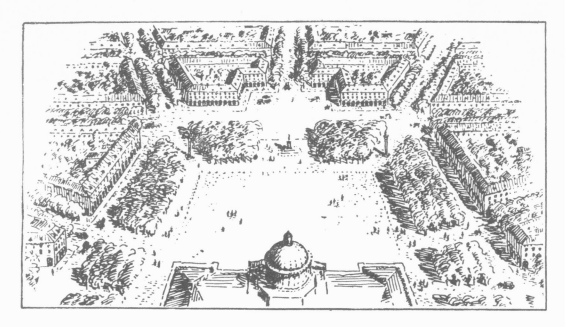

Figure 17. Landscape architect Elbert Peets drew these sketches suggesting how the east side of the Capitol grounds might have looked if L'Enfant's suggestions for arcade-covered sidewalks and an itinerary column one mile distant from the Capitol building had actually been constructed. From *On the Art of Designing Cities: Selected Essays of Elbert Peets.* Edited by Paul D. Spreiregen (Cambridge, Mass., and London, Eng.: M.I.T. Press, c1968), figures 30 and 31. *General Collections, LC.*

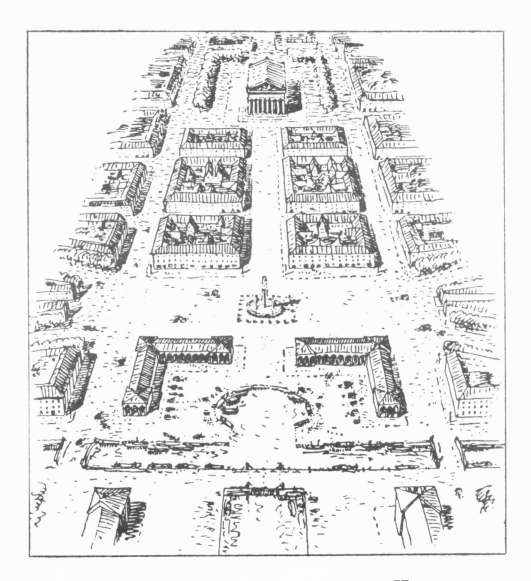

Figure 18. This sketch by Elbert Peets depicts what L'Enfant may have had in mind for 8th Street, N.W. with the canal in the foreground, a market and large plaza, and a national church or pantheon. From *On the Art of Designing Cities: Selected Essays of Elbert Peets.* Edited by Paul D. Spreiregen (Cambridge, Mass., and London, Eng.: M.I.T. Press, c1968), figure 26. *General Collections, LC.*

The letter "E" on the plan designates the locations of "Five grand fountains intended with a constant spout of water." L'Enfant notes that "There are within the limits of the City, above 25 good springs of excellent water abundantly supplied in the driest season of the year."

To encourage the States of the Union to participate in the settlement and improvement of the city, L'Enfant identified fifteen squares "for each of them to improve or subscribe a sum additional to the value of the land [for] that purpose, and the improvements round the Squares to be completed in a limited time." L'Enfant pointed out that "The Center of each Square will admit of Statues, Columns, Obelisks, or any other ornaments, such as the different States may choose to erect." Because the squares "are the most advantageously and reciprocally seen from each other, and as equally distributed over the whole City district, and connected by spacious Avenues," L'Enfant believed it likely that "The settlements round those Squares must soon be connected." The squares, numbered 1 to 15, were originally colored yellow, but are now faded to a light brown tint.

Three bridges serving the city are depicted on the plan: one across the Potomac River above Georgetown, and two crossing the Eastern Branch at the termini of East Capitol Street and Pennsylvania Avenue, S.E. A dotted line from the Virginia shore to Georgetown identifies the location of Mason's Ferry.

Fortifications are delineated on the high ground west of 23rd Street, N.W., a site now occupied by the Naval Medical Command. In addition, an elaborate facility consisting of what appears to be possible fortifications, numerous buildings (perhaps warehouses), and a breakwater are shown at the entrance to the "Canal through St. James Creek" (Fort Lesley J. McNair today). Although the use of this complex is not explained on the plan, it seems to have been intended for the major military installation designed to protect the city from an attack by water.[182] The site has long been associated with military functions. By 1794, a one-gun battery was in place and an arsenal designed by George Hadfield was constructed during the Jefferson administration.[183] The elaborate breakwater, however, suggests that L'Enfant may also have intended it as the city's distribution center for produce and merchandise, a place where sailing ships and canal boats could be safely loaded and unloaded. Certainly the protective harbor created by the breakwater at the entrance to the canal suggests this possibility. In his report to the President in June 1791, L'Enfant describes the canal as "giving entrance to the Boats from the falls of that River [i.e., Potomac] into the eastern Branch harbour."[184] Furthermore, the site is in close proximity to the wharves depicted on the plan from 7th Street, S.W. to Greenleaf Point and along the western shore of the Eastern Branch.

For some unexplained reason, L'Enfant failed to identify on his plan the site he preferred for the Judiciary, the third branch of the federal government. The unidentified building depicted at 4th Street, N.W. (Judiciary Square today) more than likely was meant for the courts. He certainly had major sites in mind for the Judiciary and other public buildings when on August 19 he described to the President how attractive the area between the President's square and the Capitol grounds would be. "the Grand avenu connecting both the palace [i.e., President's House] and the federal House [i.e., Congress House or Capitol]," he noted, "will be most magnificent and most convenient . . . and also the severals squar or area such as are Intended for the Judiciary court, the national bank—the grand church—the play House, market & Exchange . . . will offer a variety of situations unparalleled in point of beauties—suitable to Every purpose and in Every point convenient both are devised for the first asset of the city and combined to command the height [i.e., highest] price in a sale."[185] John W. Reps, in his *Monumental Washington*, points out that "The importance of this site [i.e., Judiciary Square] cannot be appreciated from a mere examination of the plan. It is on a pronounced rise in the terrain, the highest point near Pennsylvania Avenue from the Capitol to the White House."[186]

L'Enfant also did not identify the sites he had chosen for the national bank, the play house, the exchange, and the city's principal market place. Along the Eastern Branch, however, two short canals are indicated leading to markets and a broadening of the Tiber Creek Canal at 8th Street, N.W. may have been intended for a centrally located market. The latter site was subsequently developed as the city's Center Market (Figures 18 and 19).

Six blocks south of the Capitol, facing the canal, there is a large open space whose function is not clear on the plan. The space is graced by a fountain and the partial outline of a building surrounded by a brown circle. The latter is all that remains of a color tint (perhaps green) that was applied to the manuscript when it was drawn in 1791. George Walker tells us in his broadside of March 12, 1793, that the site was "intended to contain a CITY HALL, and a bason [i.e., basin] of water."[187] This is also the site of the Carroll House that L'Enfant had torn down in November 1791.

At the southern end of what was to become 8th Street, S.E., on the bank of the Eastern Branch (the Washington Navy Yard today), L'Enfant incorporated into his plan a grand open space. This may have been an afterthought on L'Enfant's

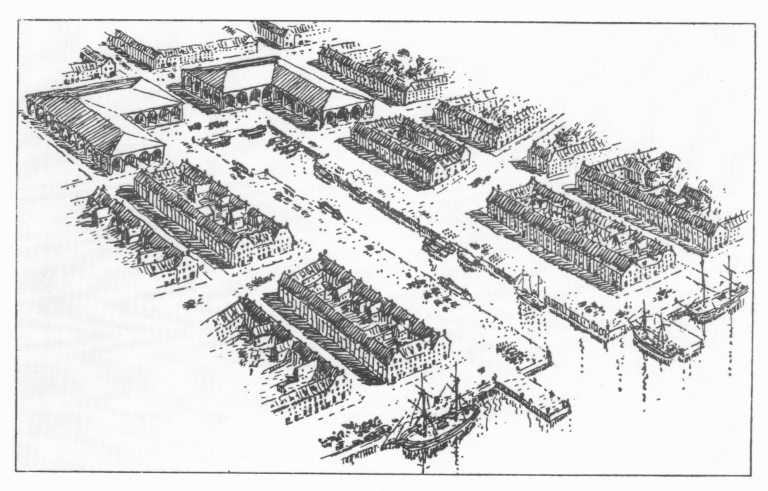

Figure 19. L'Enfant's plan depicts a quay on the Eastern Branch at 5th Street, S.E. which he identifies as a "Canal to the market." In this drawing, Elbert Peets suggests what it might have looked like if it had been built. From *On the*

Art of Designing Cities: Selected Essays of Elbert Peets. Edited by Paul D. Spreiregen (Cambridge, Mass., and London, Eng.: M.I.T. Press, c1968), figure 27. *General Collections, LC.*

part, because the plan shows clearly that streets and squares were erased to form the open space. Although not mentioned in the "References" accompanying the plan, it seems likely that it was here that L'Enfant hoped to fulfill the President's promise to the landowners on June 29 to build a "Town house, or exchange."[188] This use of the space is supported by George Walker's statement that "The AREA at the south end of East Eight Street is for the GENERAL EXCHANGE, and its public walks, &c."[189]

The map title as originally added to the L'Enfant plan may not have included an author credit line. "By Peter Charles L'Enfant" looks as though it were squeezed into the bottom of the cartouche almost as an afterthought. It is off center, at a slight angle to the rest of the lettering, and was probably written in a different hand. It may be that L'Enfant saw no reason to add his name because this copy was not for publication, but rather for the use of the President, who obviously knew it was his work. If L'Enfant's name was added later, it was probably done before the map was exhibited before both houses of Congress on December 13, 1791.

Dunlap's American Daily Advertiser for December 26, 1791, Philip Freneau's *National Gazette* for January 2, 1792, and John Fenno's *Gazette of the United States* for January 4, each include detailed descriptions of L'Enfant's plan of the new city.[190]

Each quotes in full the "description . . . annexed to the plan of the City of Washington, in the district of Columbia, as sent to Congress by the President some days ago" and all leave little doubt that the map laid before Congress was either the plan preserved today in the Library of Congress or a close copy of it.[191]

Two months later, L'Enfant's manuscript was used by Benjamin and Andrew Ellicott in the preparation of the reduced drawing for the engravers. As noted earlier in this essay, the manuscript still includes remnants of the pencil corrections which were made by Jefferson at this time for the engravers. Following this use, it was retained by the President until December 1, 1796, when he gave up custody of the plan and referred it to the care of the Commissioners.

The Plan in the Office of Public Buildings and Grounds

Changes occurred in the administrative structure of the District of Columbia, and the responsibility for public buildings and grounds eventually devolved by an act of March 2, 1867, to the Chief of Engineers of the U.S. Army. An Office of Public Buildings and Grounds under the Chief of Engineers was created, and relevant records of the Commissioners, including the L'Enfant plan, were transferred to their keeping.

By the beginning of the 1880s the condition of the L'Enfant plan had deteriorated greatly. In an article about a proposed memorial to L'Enfant appearing in the May 31, 1884, edition of the Washington *Evening Star*, the reporter includes this vivid description of "a time-stained and tattered paper in the possession of Architect Clarke":

> Thrown in carelessly among a mass of maps and plans in the gloomy little basement room occupied by the architect of the Capitol, has lain, for years, the original plan of Washington, drawn by L'Enfant in 1790, from which Andrew Ellicott's plan was made in 1792. . . . L'Enfant's plan was never engraved and is yellow and worn with age. The lines marking the lots have paled until they are almost invisible. In half a dozen places it has been torn and certain colors of ink maintained on the margin have disappeared entirely. The plot itself is elegantly gotten up, the writing is like copper-plate, and the whole work is as beautiful as that of a counterfeiter.[192]

In this article the reporter implies that the L'Enfant plan was in the custody of Architect of the Capitol Clarke. The records of the Office of Public Buildings and Grounds were stored in the Capitol basement from before 1867 to 1884, when they were moved to the Winder Building on 17th Street, N.W.[193] More than likely, the records he saw were those belonging to the Office of Public Buildings and Grounds rather than to the Architect.

In a letter endorsed March 19, 1887, Col. John Wilson, head of the Office of Public Buildings and Grounds, remarked that the L'Enfant plan was "in a dilapidated condition," adding, "I called attention to it in my annual reports for 1885 & 1886 and asked for an appropriation for copying it."[194] Colonel Wilson stressed that "It is a map of great value and importance" and "is constantly called for by attorneys and frequently by the courts."[195]

The Coast and Geodetic Survey Makes a Tracing

Pressure to make a reproducible copy of the L'Enfant plan reached a decisive level in early 1887 due to the federal government's involvement in a suit before the Supreme Court of the District of Columbia concerning the ownership of the Potomac River tidal flats. With the assistance of the Attorney General, arrangements were made for the temporary transfer of this precious but fragile document to the U.S. Coast and Geodetic Survey for the purpose of making an accurate tracing suitable for reproduction and submission as evidence in a suit of law.

The Coast and Geodetic Survey (now the National Ocean Service of the National Oceanic and Atmospheric Administration) was a natural choice for this undertaking. The Survey, universally recognized as the U.S. government's finest scientific agency, employed a corps of some twenty-six experienced and skilled topographic draughtsmen capable of performing this difficult assignment.

B. A. Colonna, head of the Survey's Office of Topography, noted that when he received the manuscript for copying, it "was in a dilapidated state; it had been mounted on cotton cloth and varnished (evidently many years ago) for preservation, by which it had been rendered quite opaque. It was cracked in some places and otherwise defaced, and its faded condition required the work of reproduction, revision, comparison, and final verification to be done under special conditions of solar light reflected by mirrors and with the aid of magnifying glasses and color screens."[196]

The tracing was promptly completed and the first reproductions in black and white were issued on May 20, 1887. Blue, green, yellow, light red, and dark red tints were subsequently added to the lithographed facsimile to conform to the explanatory notes or the vestiges of color found on the original plan (Figure 20). Until the Library of Congress' colored facsimile reproduction and the accompanying enhanced digitized image were issued a little over one hundred years later, the Coast and Geodetic Survey's facsimile was the only full-size reproduction available for sale to the public.

Their work on the plan finished, the Coast and Geodetic Survey returned the L'Enfant manuscript on September 26, 1887, along with several copies of the facsimile, to the Office of Public Buildings and Grounds.

The Plan Is Transferred to the Library of Congress

In September 1918, Col. C. S. Ridley, then in charge of the Office of Public Buildings and Grounds, became alarmed about the continuing deterioration of the L'Enfant plan in his custody and the general lack of suitable fireproof conditions in the Lemon Building in which his offices were situated. On September 26, he expressed his concerns in a letter to the Librarian of Congress and sought his advice. "While the map is still quite legible," he wrote, "it appears to be fading and disintegrating; furthermore, the floor on which this office is housed is far from fireproof. While I am not prepared to relinquish title to the map, it occurred to me that it would be possible, and appeal to you as desirable, to deposit it for safekeeping in the Library of Congress; and perhaps even, while in such custody, to have it restored should that prove advisable."[197]

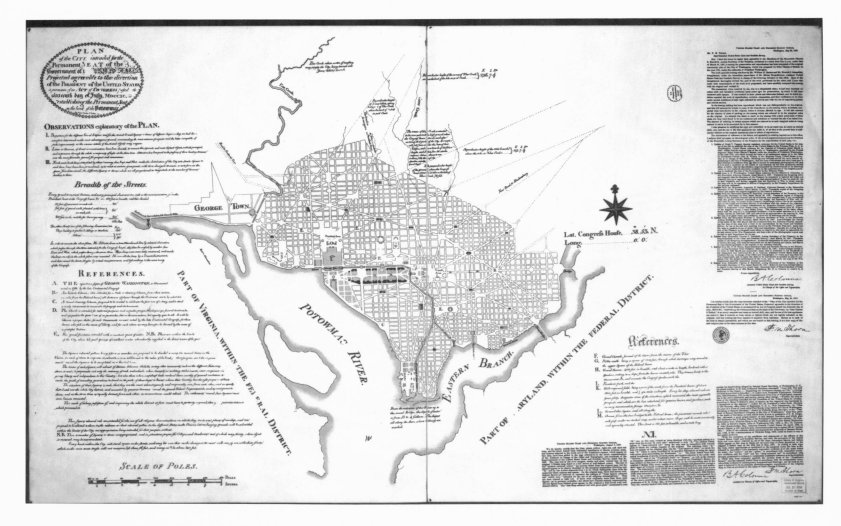

Figure 20. Facsimile reproduction of the L'Enfant plan of the city of Washington, made in 1887 by the Coast and Geodetic Survey (now the National Ocean Service). *Geography and Map Division, LC.*

Acting Librarian of Congress A. P. C. Griffin responded affirmatively two days later. He wrote that "the Library of Congress would be pleased to receive the L'Enfant map of Washington, as a deposit for safe-keeping, subject to withdrawal by you or your successor in office. If deposited in the Library, the Map would be protected against further disintegration; also it would be cleaned and restored. In all ways it would be treated with the consideration due to an historical document of very high value."[198]

On November 4, Colonel Ridley notified the Library that he would "be glad to send the map to you at such time as may be convenient for you to receive it. It is now enclosed in a small wooden box, arranged to be opened readily like the covers of a book."[199]

The map was picked up by the Library's wagon on November 11 and delivered to the Manuscript Division. A few days later the L'Enfant plan was transferred to the custody of the Division of Maps. An obviously delighted chief of the Division of Maps informed the Librarian of Congress on November 16 that "This is the most important accession of local interest transferred to the Division of Map[s], and will always be considered as the most valuable local accession to this Division."[200] Division Chief Philip Lee Phillips gave credit to Charles Moore, Acting Chief of the Manuscript Division, who, appar-ently working behind the scenes, was responsible for the transfer. "Mr. Moore's efforts," wrote Phillips, "will receive the utmost appreciation, not only of the Library of Congress, but of all lovers of material of local interest."[201]

Since its receipt in the Library in 1918, the L'Enfant manuscript plan has been considered an honored cartographic treasure. Its use and display, however, have been carefully monitored because of its brittle condition, the darkness of the paper due to the varnish placed on its surface in the nineteenth century, and the fear of addi-tional fading of its already faint street pattern. In fact the plan has not been publicly displayed for an extended period of time since November 1966, when the Library of Congress, in conjunction with the President's Temporary Commission on Pennsylvania Avenue, mounted a major exhibi-tion entitled "The Grand Design." Over the years, inquiries received in the Library's Geography and Map Reading Room to study the plan and requests for photoreproductions have been sat-isfied by using the full-size tracing published in 1887 by the Coast and Geodetic Survey.

The 1951 Restoration of the Plan

The first major attempt to repair and restore the L'Enfant plan was made in 1951, when the Library of Congress hired the well-known document restorer Evelyn Ehrlich, formerly of Harvard University's Fogg Art Museum, to undertake the difficult assignment. Mrs. Ehrlich painstakingly removed the paper and cloth on which the map had been mounted many years previously. Tears and breaks were carefully mended with paper fibers and the map surface was examined to determine if it would be feasible to reduce the discoloration or brown stain. It subsequently was decided not to attempt to remove or lighten the brown color because of the possibility of damage to the map image as well as to the remaining traces of watercolor wash. In order to improve the general appearance of the plan, however, Mrs. Ehrlich inpainted the erased portions of map surface to conform to the overall background color of the document. The map was not remounted on linen or paper at that time but was matted and placed in a simple wooden frame with a sheet of Plexiglas over the viewing surface.

The Physical Condition of the Plan

A little more than a decade ago, the L'Enfant plan and other early plans and maps of Washington, D.C., prepared in the Surveyor's Office were the subjects of examination and study, with the results being incorporated into three articles published in the Summer 1979 issue of *The Quarterly Journal of the Library of Congress*.[202] The renewed historical interest in L'Enfant's manuscript plan also led to a comprehensive study of its physical condition by Marian Dirda of the Library's Conservation Office. In her report dated January 6, 1981, in which she detailed what "major" and "minor" treatment of the plan might entail, Dirda noted that "Major conservation would undoubtedly make the paper more flexible and chemically stable." In addition, "It would also probably improve the visibility of the image by washing away the discolored glue coating," but she warned that "major treatment could cause the loss of some information on the creation and history of the map of interest to future scholars." Certainly, if an attempt had been made to remove the varnish (i.e., glue) coating when the map was last restored in 1951, it is likely that Jefferson's editorial notations would have been inadvertently lost during the treatment. In a memorandum accompanying Marian Dirda's report, Conservation Officer Peter Waters suggested that "Before any decision is made concerning any treatment action, . . . a first class facsimile [be] made, which could serve as the reader service copy."[203]

Because of the possible loss of information, only critical minor repairs were authorized and completed at the time. Pressure sensitive tape was removed from the back of the plan, detached pieces were reattached, and some tears were mended with Japanese paper and paste. As a temporary measure, the plan was inserted into a polyester film envelope and placed in a plain, gray metal frame between two sheets of Plexiglas.

The Washington, D.C., Map Project

In 1987, the treatment, reproduction, and storage of the L'Enfant plan became the cornerstone of a much broader, four-year joint program instituted by the Library of Congress and the National Geographic Society. With the bicentennial anniversaries of the planning, initial construction, and occupancy of the city to occur between the years 1991 and 2000, a broad program was put into motion which would preserve and make known the superb collection of official and commercially produced maps and atlases of Washington, D.C., in the Library of Congress collections. The program was made possible in part by a generous gift of $348,250 from the National Geographic Society.

As initially defined, the program was divided into six basic parts: (1) to catalog and classify all maps and atlases of Washington, D.C., in the Geography and Map Division and input this information into the Library's automated data base; (2) to prepare a cartobibliography describing in detail the maps of the City from 1790 to 1910; (3) to publish a quality facsimile reproduction of the L'Enfant plan, "followed by treatment that will restore the former integrity of the map;" (4) to accomplish the overall restoration of the Washington, D.C., map and atlas collections and the microfilming of each object; (5) to compile and publish a historical atlas of maps of Washington, D.C.; and (6) to host a symposium and exhibition in 1991 focusing on the planning and mapping of the City.[204]

Photographing the Plan

Soon after the joint program was instituted, advice was sought from several government agencies concerning how to obtain photographs of the L'Enfant plan that would be of sufficient quality to be used in producing a clear, full-color facsimile reproduction. Because of the near illegibility of parts of the original document, particularly the street pattern which had been drawn in pencil, these discussions eventually led to suggestions of employing "state of the art" computer enhancement technology. It was felt that by digitizing the plan, the background clutter (i.e., the varnish) could be suppressed and the illegible street pattern enhanced, thereby producing an image similar to what it looked like in

1791. After studying this issue, officials of the U.S. Geological Survey's Eastern Mapping Center, viewing the L'Enfant plan as an excellent test of their skill in applying automation to difficult cartographic problems, agreed to photograph the document on one of their large mapping cameras and to conduct a test to determine the feasibility of producing an enhanced digitized image.

A specially designed carrying case was made to protect the L'Enfant plan and, on three occasions in 1988, the document was taken to the Geological Survey's headquarters in Reston, Virginia, to be photographed. Eastern Mapping Center photographer Jon Foreman made a full-size black-and-white film negative using high contrast panchromatic film, as well as 8- by 10-inch color negatives and color transparencies.

The Enhanced Digitized Image

Employing a Scitex rotating drum raster scanner and edit station, approximately 10 percent of the film negative was scanned, the image enhanced, and the results plotted on film and then reproduced on paper for study by Geological Survey and Library of Congress officials. The prototype was prepared by Eastern Mapping Center cartographer William Schinkel working under the direction of supervisory cartographer Eileen F. Doughty. The test clearly demonstrated

that automation could be used to restore most of the drawing's original legibility while eliminating unwanted background clutter. Based on the success of the feasibility study and with the cost being shared by the Library of Congress, the National Geographic Society, the National Park Service, and the Geological Survey, the last agency commenced the complete digitizing and enhancement of the L'Enfant plan in May 1990, finishing the undertaking on July 8, 1991.[205]

The Facsimile Reproduction

Concurrent with the Geological Survey's preparation of the digitized image, work began on a full-color facsimile reproduction of the L'Enfant plan. Color Masters Enterprises, Inc., Alexandria, Virginia, first using the color transparency made in 1988 by the Geological Survey and subsequently replacing it with a new transparency prepared by photographer Edward Owen, successfully produced the high quality color separations needed for printing the facsimile. On August 26, 1991, the two hundreth anniversary of Pierre L'Enfant's presentation of his plan of the nation's capital to President Washington, the Library of Congress published an exact-size, full-color facsimile and a computer-assisted reproduction of the original manuscript plan preserved in the Library of Congress. These reproductions are the first to be based on photography and electronic enhancement technology.[206]

The Preservation and Framing

With the publication of the facsimile and the computer-assisted reproduction, conservator Marian Dirda undertook the final preservation treatment of L'Enfant's fragile manuscript. Treatment consisted of removing or thinning the white paper reinforcing strips placed on the verso in 1951 to protect the edges of the document, but now the source of small cracks in the brittle eighteenth-century paper; removing the thick hide glue residues along the upper and lower front edges; lightening the dark inpainting applied during the earlier restoration; and filling losses with western paper and mending unrepaired tears with Japanese paper and paste. At the conclusion of the treatment, the plan was placed in a hermetically sealed case containing argon gas. The container was designed especially for the L'Enfant plan by Dr. Robert E. McComb of the Library's Preservation Research and Testing Office. In this environment the plan will be protected for decades to come from further chemical and atmospheric degradation as well as from damage that might be caused by careless handling. On the occasion of its two hundredth anniversary, all that is prudent has been done to preserve, protect, and make known this revered cartographic treasure.

Notes

1. Broadside Collection, Portfolio 179, no. 15, Copy 1, Rare Book and Special Collections Division, LC. Members of the committee were Robert Peter, George Walker, Bernard O'Nell, Benjamin Stoddert, and William Deakins, Jr. from Georgetown and George Gilpin, John Fitzgerald, Charles Simms, David Stuart, and Robert T. Hooe from Alexandria. See Donald Sweig, "A Capital on the Potomac: A 1789 Broadside and Alexandria's Attempts to Capture the Cherished Prize," *The Virginia Magazine of History and Biography* 87 (Jan. 1979):74–104.

2. Dumas Malone, *Jefferson and His Time*, 6 vols. (Boston: Little, Brown and Co., 1948–1981), vol. 2, *Jefferson and the Rights of Man*, 292.

3. "The Assumption," [1792?] Papers of Thomas Jefferson, series 1, reel 13, Manuscript Division, LC (hereafter cited as Jefferson Papers); *The Papers of Thomas Jefferson*, Julian P. Boyd, ed. (Princeton, N.J.: Princeton University Press, 1950–), 17:207 (hereafter cited as *The Papers of Thomas Jefferson*).

4. Kenneth R. Bowling, *Creating the Federal City, 1774–1800: Potomac Fever* (Washington: The American Institute of Architects Press, 1988), 75. Bowling states that "On 22

June, Hamilton informed several of his Massachusetts supporters that assumption would be added to the funding bill if a Philadelphia-Potomac residence bill passed Congress first. What Hamilton wanted from the Massachusetts congressmen was a promise that they would not, as in 1789, support efforts to block the Philadelphia-Potomac scheme with a counteroffer to Pennsylvania."

5. "An Act for Establishing the Temporary and Permanent seat of the Government of the United States," Section 1, *United States Statutes at Large* (Boston: Charles C. Little and James Brown, 1845–   ), 1:130.

6. Bowling, *Creating the Federal City*, 78.

7. "Proceedings to be had under the Residence act," 29 August 1790, Jefferson Papers, series 1, reel 12; *The Papers of Thomas Jefferson*, 17:460–461.

8. Ibid.

9. Ibid.

10. Ibid.

11. Ibid.

12. Jefferson identifies the landowner simply as "our host." Boyd in *The Papers of Thomas Jefferson* (17:467) states that "our host" is George Mason of Gunston Hall. Others, for example, Saul K. Padover, ed., *Thomas Jefferson and the National Captial* (Washington: U.S. Government Printing Office, 1946), 28, have suggested that it was John Mason. John Mason, however, was in France and did not return to the United States until midsummer 1791. See Helen Hill Miller, *George Mason Gentleman Revolutionary* (Chapel Hill: University of North Carolina Press, 1975), 318.

13. Jefferson to Washington, 17 September 1790, Papers of George Washington, series 4, reel 99, Manuscript Division, LC (hereafter cited as Washington Papers); *The Papers of Thomas Jefferson*, 17:466.

14. Jefferson's report to Washington on meeting held at Georgetown, 14 September 1790, Jefferson Papers, series 3, reel 57; *The Papers of Thomas Jefferson*, 17:461–462.

15. Ibid., 17:462.

16. Ibid., 17:463.

17. Ibid.

18. *The Times, and Patowmack Packet* ([Georgetown, Md.], no. 88, 20 October 1790):3.

19. "Offer by Citizens of Georgetown," October 13, 1790, in Allen C. Clark, "Origin of the Federal City," *Records of the Columbia Historical Society* 35–36 (1935):23.

20. Samuel Davidson to Robert Dunlop, 28 November 1790, Samuel Davidson Papers, Letter book, Manuscript Division, LC.

21. Wilhelmus B. Bryan, *A History of the National Capital from Its Foundation Through the Period of the Adoption of the Organic Act*, 2 vols. (New York: Macmillan Co., 1914–16), 1:120–123; *Dictionary of American Biography*, 20 vols. and index (New York: Charles Scribner's Sons, 1928–1937), 3:523–524 and 10:121–122.

22. "An Act for Establishing the Temporary and Permanent Seat of the Government of the United States," Section 2, *United States Statutes at Large*, 1:130.

23. Ibid., Section 3.

24. "Proclamation," 24 January 1791, Washington Papers, series 4, reel 100; *The Writings of George Washington*, ed. John C. Fitzpatrick, 39 vols. (Westport, Conn.: Greenwood Press, 1970), 31:203 (hereafter cited as *Writings of George Washington*).

25. Washington to the Senate and House of Representatives, 24 January, 1791, Washington Papers, series 4, reel 100; *Writings of George Washington*, 31:201.

26. The name "Tiber" may have been first used for this stream in the previous century. Constance Green, in her *Washington: A History of the Capital 1800–1950* (Princeton, N.J.: Princeton University Press, 1976), 5, writes that "A man named Pope had owned that land in the seventeenth century and, having called his plantation 'Rome,' had christened the brook 'Tiber.' " L'Enfant's plan of the city (August 1791) and subsequent manuscript and printed maps use the name "Tiber Creek."

27. James F. Duhamel, "Tiber Creek," *Records of the Columbia Historical Society* 28 (1962):215.

28. [Tobias Lear] *Observations on the River Potomack, the Country Adjacent, and the City of Washington* (New York: Samuel Loudon and Son, 1793), 18.

29. L'Enfant to Washington, 11 September 1789, Washington Papers, series 7, reel 120.

30. Hans Paul Caemmerer, *The Life of Pierre Charles L'Enfant, Planner of the City Beautiful, The City of Washington* (Washington: National Republic Publishing Co., 1950), 1. Caemmerer's work is the best account of the life of L'Enfant. See also "Pierre Charles L'Enfant" written by Fiske Kimball in *Dictionary of American Biography*, 11:165–169.

31. Certificate appointing L'Enfant Captain of Engineers in the U.S. Army dated February 18, 1778, and witnessed and signed April 13, 1779; certificate of promotion from Captain to "Major by Brevet," May 2, 1783; and certificate of exchange, January 2, 1782. Digges-L'Enfant Morgan Papers, box 1, Manuscript Division, LC (hereafter cited as Digges-L'Enfant-Morgan Papers).

32. Hugh T. Taggart, "Old Georgetown," *Records of the Columbia Historical Society* 11 (1908):216.

33. Sally Kennedy Alexander, "A Sketch of the Life of Major Andrew Ellicott," *Records of the Columbia Historical Society* 2 (1899):175.

34. Ibid., 170–171, Jefferson to Ellicott, 2 February 1791.

35. Washington to L'Enfant, 13 December 1791, Washington Papers, series 4, reel 101; *Writings of George Washington*, 31:443.

36. Jefferson to L'Enfant, March 1791, Digges-L'Enfant-Morgan Papers, box 1; Saul K. Padover, ed., *Thomas Jefferson and the National Capital* (Washington: U.S. Government Printing Office, 1946), 42–43.

37. Washington to William Deakins, Jr. and Benjamin Stoddert, 3 February 1791, Washington Papers, series 2, reel 9; *Writings of George Washington*, 31:208.

38. Washington to Deakins and Stoddert, 2 March 1791, Washington Papers, series 4, reel 100; *Writings of George Washington*. 31:227.

39. Proclamation, 30 March 1791, Jefferson Papers, series 1, reel 14. Jefferson draft has pencil date of March 31, 1791 written in later hand; *Writings of George Washington*, 31:255, footnote 13.

40. Jefferson Papers, box 24, folder Mar. 20–31, 1791 (B), no. 10805.

41. References "H" and "K" on L'Enfant's "Plan of the City, intended for the Permanent Seat of the Government of the United States," [August 1791].

42. See "[Maps of Landholdings in the Part of Prince George's County (Md.) that is Now Central Washington,

D.C.]" by Charles Beatty and Archibald Orme, surveyors. [179-] 2 ms. maps. G3851 .G46 s19 .B4 Vault, Geography and Map Division, LC.

43. Silvio A. Bedini, *The Life of Benjamin Banneker* (New York: Charles Scribner's Sons, 1972), 122–123. Bedini indicates that there are no copies extant of the March 12th issue of *The Georgetown Weekly Ledger*, but it was reprinted in other newspapers, such as *The Maryland Gazette*, 18 March 1791.

44. Alexander, "A Sketch of the Life of Major Andrew Ellicott," 172.

45. L'Enfant to Jefferson, 11 March, 1791, Digges-L'Enfant-Morgan Papers, box 1; *The Papers of Thomas Jefferson*, 20:77.

46. Ibid.

47. Ibid.

48. Ibid. The "heights" dominating Georgetown include Mount Alto at Wisconsin Avenue and Calvert Street and Mount St. Albans at Massachusetts and Wisconsin Avenues.

49. Jefferson to L'Enfant, 17 March 1791, Digges-L'Enfant-Morgan Papers, box 1; *The Papers of Thomas Jefferson*, 20:80.

50. Ibid.

51. L'Enfant to Jefferson, 20 March 1791, Jefferson Papers, series 3, reel 57; *The Papers of Thomas Jefferson*, 20:81.

52. *The Diaries of George Washington, 1748–1799*, ed. John C. Fitzpatrick, 4 vols. (Boston and New York: Houghton Mifflin Co., 1925), 4:153 (hereafter cited as *Diaries of George Washington*).

53. L'Enfant to Jefferson, 4 April, 1791, Jefferson Papers, series 3, reel 57; *The Papers of Thomas Jefferson*, 20:83.

54. "Note relative to the Ground laying on the Eastern branch of the River Potowmack & being Intended to parallel the severals position proposed within the limits between tha[t] branch & Georgetown for the Seat of the Federal City," [26 March 1791], Papers of Pierre Charles L'Enfant, Manuscript Division, LC (hereafter cited as L'Enfant Papers). Endorsed on page 8, "Report on the District of Columbia as Suitable for a City by L'Enfant. 1. No. 1. (PB&G) 1791. *Enclosure.*" Note attached to the report states that "The above was personally handed to the Executive on his arrival at Georgetown at that time."

55. Ibid., 1–2.

56. Ibid., 5.

57. Ibid., 6.

58. Ibid., 5–6.

59. Ibid., 6–7.

60. Ibid., 4.

61. Ibid., 8.

62. "Observations explanatory of the Plan," no. II, on L'Enfant's "Plan of the City, intended for the Permanent Seat of the Government of the United States," [August 1791].

63. William T. Partridge, *L'Enfant's Methods and Features of His Plan for the Federal City. Excerpt from the "Annual Report, National Capital Park and Planning Commission, 1930"* (Washington: National Capital Planning Commission [January 1975]), 1.

64. L'Enfant to Jefferson, 4 April 1791, Jefferson Papers, series 3, reel 57; *The Papers of Thomas Jefferson*, 20:83.

65. *Diaries of George Washington*, 4:153.

66. Ibid., 4:154.

67. Ibid.

68. Ibid.

69. L'Enfant to Jefferson, 4 April 1791, Jefferson Papers, series 3, reel 57; *The Papers of Thomas Jefferson*, 20:83.

70. *Diaries of George Washington*, 4:154.

71. Washington to Jefferson, 31 March 1791, Jefferson Papers, General Correspondence, series 2, reel 14; *Writings of George Washington*, 31:256–257.

72. Ibid.

73. *Diaries of George Washington*, 4:155.

74. Washington to L'Enfant, 4 April 1791, Digges-L'Enfant-Morgan Papers, box 1; *Writings of George Washington*, 31:270.

75. Ibid.

76. Ibid., 31:271.

77. Ibid.

78. Although Clarke's plan is no longer extant, a four-page proposal for a "new city," signed by Joseph Clarke, is included in the Digges-L'Enfant-Morgan Papers, box 1. The notes originally accompanied the plan.

79. Washington to L'Enfant, 4 April 1791, Digges-L'Enfant-Morgan Papers, box 1; *Writings of George Washington*, 31:271.

80. L'Enfant to Jefferson, 4 April 1791, Jefferson Papers, series 3, reel 57; *The Papers of Thomas Jefferson*, 20:83.

81. Ibid. 20:84.

82. Jefferson to L'Enfant, 10 April 1791, Digges-L'Enfant-Morgan Papers, box 1; *The Papers of Thomas Jefferson*, 20:83.

83. Ibid.

84. Ibid.

85. Ibid.

86. John Trumbull, *Autobiography, Reminiscences and Letters* (New York and London: Wiley and Putnam; New Haven: B. L. Hamlen, 1841), 166.

87. *Journal of William Loughton Smith, 1790–1791*, ed. Albert Matthews (Cambridge, Mass.: The University Press, 1917), 62.

88. Daniel Carroll to James Madison, 23 April 1791, Papers of James Madison, series 1, reel 4, Manuscript Division, LC (hereafter cited as Madison Papers); Elizabeth S. Kite, *L'Enfant and Washington, 1791–1792* (Baltimore: The Johns Hopkins Press, 1929), 50–51.

89. L'Enfant to Washington, 22 June 1791, 1, L'Enfant Papers. The "Incompleat drawing" is no longer extant, but two versions of the report have survived, one in L'Enfant's handwriting and the other in the hand of his assistant Isaac Roberdeau. The latter is in the Digges-L'Enfant-Morgan Papers. Quotations in the essay are from the version in L'Enfant's hand.

90. Ibid., 2.

91. Ibid.

92. Ibid.

93. Ibid., 3.

94. Ibid., 4.

95. Ibid., 7.

96. Ibid.

97. Ibid.

98. Ibid., 5.

99. Ibid.

100. Ibid., 6.

101. Ibid.

102. *Diaries of George Washington*, 4:200.

103. Ibid., 4:200–201.

104. L'Enfant to Washington, 19 August 1791, 1, L'Enfant Papers, oversize cabinet 2, drawer 1. LC has an anonymous eighteenth-century manuscript map which depicts a pattern of streets in the nation's capital by a series of dotted lines. In 1930, Colonel Lawrence Martin, then chief of the Division of Maps expressed the opinion that the manuscript was the "map of doted lines" annexed to L'Enfant's report of August 19. See *Report of the Librarian of Congress for the Fiscal Year Ending June 30, 1930* (Washington: Government Printing Office, 1930, 164–167). It seems more likely, however, that this is the map that L'Enfant requested Benjamin Ellicott to make sometime in December 1791 to show the current status of their field work.

105. Ibid., 2.

106. Ibid.

107. Ibid., 1–2. Washington later informed L'Enfant that "As there is a suspension at present, of the business which took Mr. [Andrew] Ellicots brother to Georgia, there will be no occasion for his proceeding thither, until he shall receive further advice from me, or from the Department of War." See Washington to L'Enfant, 28 November 1791, Digges-L'Enfant-Morgan Papers, box 1; *Writings of George Washington*, 31:431.

108. Ibid., 3.

109. Ibid., 4.

110. Washington Papers, series 4, reel 100; *The Papers of Thomas Jefferson*, 22:89–90. These questions written in Washington's hand were used by Jefferson and Madison in their meeting with the Commissioners in Georgetown. On the same sheet of paper, Jefferson wrote the answers to the questions plus added seven more decisions reached at the September 8, 1791, meeting with the Commissioners.

111. Jefferson to Madison, 26 August 1791, Madison Papers, series 1, reel 5; *The Papers of Thomas Jefferson*, 22:77.

112. Jefferson to Commissioners, 28 August 1791, Jefferson Papers, series 1, reel 57; *The Papers of Thomas Jefferson*, 22:88.

113. Tobias Lear to L'Enfant, 27 August 1791, and Jefferson to L'Enfant, 31 August 1791. Digges-L'Enfant-Morgan Papers, box 1.

114. Jefferson to L'Enfant, 18 August 1791, Digges-L'Enfant-Morgan Papers, box 1; *The Papers of Thomas Jefferson*, 22:48.

115. Stephen Hallet to James Dermott, 25 January 1794, Washington Papers, series 4, reel 105.

116. Lear to L'Enfant, 6 October 1791, Digges-L'Enfant-Morgan Papers, box 1; Caemmerer, *Life of Pierre Charles L'Enfant*, 169, 171.

117. L'Enfant to Lear, 18 October 1791, 3, Digges-L'Enfant-Morgan Papers, box 1; Caemmerer, *Life of Pierre Charles L'Enfant*, 174.

118. Ibid.

119. Washington to David Stuart, 20 November 1791, Washington Papers, series 4, reel 101; *Writings of George Washington*, 31:421.

120. Ibid.

121. For a discussion of this dispute see Bryan, *A History of the National Capital*, 1:165–167.

122. Washington to Daniel Carroll of Duddington, 28 November 1791, Washington Papers, series 2, reel 9; *Writings of George Washington*, 31:430.

123. Washington to L'Enfant, 28 November 1791, Digges-L'Enfant-Morgan Papers, box 1; *Writings of George Washington*, 31:431.

124. Records of the Commissioners for the District of Columbia, *Proceedings, 1791–1802*, 25 November 1791, Record Group 42, National Archives (hereafter cited as Commissioners Records (RG42)).

125. Washington to Jefferson, 30 November 1791, Washington Papers, series 4, reel 101; *Writings of George Washington*, 31:432.

126. Washington to L'Enfant, 2 December 1791, Digges-L'Enfant-Morgan Papers, box 1. Madison's involvement is indicated in Jefferson's letter to Washington dated December 1, 1791, Jefferson Papers, series 1, reel 15; *The Papers of Thomas Jefferson*, 22:367.

127. Washington to L'Enfant, 28 November 1791, Digges-L'Enfant-Morgan Papers, box 1; *Writings of George Washington*, 31:431. The second sale of lots subsequently was postponed until October 8, 1792.

128. L'Enfant to Lear, 17 February 1792, 5, Digges-L'Enfant-Morgan Papers, box 1.

129. Ibid.

130. Ibid., 6.

131. Ibid.

132. L'Enfant was under the impression that Lear had retrieved the drawing from Pigalle. This does not seem to be the case. In a letter dated January 24, 1794, Hallet informed James Dermott that "Being called upon by the Comms. to examine a fragment of a plan in their Office I acknowledged that which has been laid before me to be the same Reduction of Maj. L'Enfants Plan of the City, which I once undertook at his Requisition from a great Map he intrusted to me and as the Reduction was intended for the use of Mr. Pigalle a French engraver, who has agreed with Maj. L'Enfant for the engraving of the same It was drawn on silk Paper in order to save Time but Maj. L'Enfant being at a Hurry took back his original before the Reduction coud be finished and I delivered it in the same State to Mr. Lear upon his application in the Name of the President." Stephen Hallet to James Dermott, January 25, 1794. Washington Papers, series 4, reel 105. The Hallet drawing apparently no longer exists. It was in the files of the Surveyor's Office of Washington, D.C., on May 31, 1802. On that date Robert King prepared an "Inventory of Books, Plans, Instruments, &, belonging to the Public in the Surveyors Office," in which he lists "Major L'Enfants old plan by Hallet." MMC, oversize cabinet 2, drawer 6, Manuscript Division, LC.

133. L'Enfant to Lear, 17 February 1792, 6, Digges-L'Enfant-Morgan Papers, box 1.

134. Ibid., 7.

135. Washington to Jefferson, 15 February 1792, Jefferson Papers, series 1, reel 15; *Writings of George Washington*, 31:480.

136. The date of receipt is derived from Andrew Ellicott's letter to the Commissioners dated February 23, 1792, in which he states that the map was handed to the President "last Monday," Commissioners Records (RG42), Letters Received, 1:81.

137. Washington to Jefferson, 22 February 1792, Jefferson Papers, series 1, reel 15; *Writings of George Washington*, 31:482–483.

138. Ibid., 31:483.

139. Samuel Davidson to George Washington, 27 November 1797, Samuel Davidson Papers, Letterbook, Manuscript Division, LC.

140. Andrew Ellicott to Commissioners, 1 January 1793, Commissioners Records (RG42), Letters Received.

141. Andrew Ellicott to Commissioners, 10 December 1791, Commissioners Records (RG42), Letters Received.

142. Andrew Ellicott to Commissioners, 23 February 1792, Commissioners Records (RG42), Letters Received, 1:81.

143. Ibid.

144. Ibid.

145. The two Americans were James Thackara and John Vallance and the Frenchman was Nareisse Pigalle, all of Philadelphia.

146. Andrew Ellicott to Commissioners, 23 February 1792, Commissioners Records (RG42), Letters Received, 1:81.

147. L'Enfant to Lear, 17 February 1792, 7, Digges-L'Enfant-Morgan Papers, box 1.

148. Washington to Commissioners, 1 December 1796, Washington Papers, series 4, reel 110; *Writings of George Washington*, 35:305.

149. The note reading, in part, "Avenue a mile long. . ." was not incorporated into the published map. In addition, the paragraph describing the "Breadth of Streets" was rewritten.

150. Washington to Jefferson, 4 March 1792, Jefferson Papers, series 1, reel 15; *Writings of George Washington*, 31:495.

151. Ibid.

152. Ibid.

153. Frederick R. Goff, "The Federal City in 1793," *Library of Congress Quarterly Journal of Current Acquisitions* 9 (Nov. 1951): 6. Reprinted in *A la Carte: Selected Papers on Maps and Atlases*, comp. Walter W. Ristow (Washington: Library of Congress, 1972), 148.

154. Thackara and Vallance's copperplate has survived and is on permanent exhibition in the display center of the National Ocean Service, Rockville, Maryland.

155. The Hill engraving concludes with 22nd Street East and square no. 1136, whereas the Thackara and Vallance engraving extends the plan eastward to 25th Street East and includes 1146 numbered squares.

156. Commissioners to L'Enfant, 9 September 1791, Commissioners Records (RG42), Letters Sent, 1:32-33. It is not known who at this meeting suggested that the city be named for George Washington. More than likely, however, Jefferson and Madison had decided this in advance of the meeting. It probably was generally accepted that some version of his name would be used. As early as April 22, 1791, Representative William Loughton Smith (S.C.) proposed to L'Enfant "calling this new Seat of Empire, Washingtonople." See *Journal of William Loughton Smith, 1790–1791*, ed. Albert Mathews (Cambridge, Mass.: The University Press, 1917), 62.

157. "Report of a Committee Appointed to Choose Names for Richmond City Streets, Submitted to Council 14 June 1798," Archives Division, Virginia State Library,

Richmond, Va., no. 18615; Harry M. Ward and Harold E. Greer, Jr., *Richmond During the Revolution, 1775–83* (Charlottesville: Published for the Richmond Independence Bicentennial Commission by the University Press of Virginia, 1977), 42.

158. Andrew Ellicott to Commissioners, 10 December 1791, Commissioners Records (RG42), Letters Received.

159. Pamela Scott, " 'This Vast Empire': The Iconography of the Mall, 1791–1848," in *The Mall in Washington, 1791–1991*, Richard Longstreth, ed. (Washington: National Gallery of Art, 1991), 39–40.

160. George Walker, "A Description of the Situation and Plan of the City of Washington Now Building for the Metropolis of America, and Established as the Permanent Residence of Congress After the Year 1800" (London: March 12, 1793). Broadside. Geography and Map Division, LC, G3850 1793 .W3 Vault.

161. Washington to Jefferson, 22 February 1792, Jefferson Papers, series 1, reel 115; *Writings of George Washington*, 31:483.

162. Washington to L'Enfant, 28 February 1792, Digges-L'Enfant-Morgan Papers, box 1; *Writings of George Washington*, 31:489.

163. Caemmerer, *Life of Pierre Charles L'Enfant*, 193–198; Ellicott to Commissioners, 23 February 1792, Commissioners Records (RG42), Letters Received, 1:81.

164. Ellicott to Commissioners, 23 February 1792, Commissioners Records (RG42), Letters Received, 1:81.

165. Washington to Stuart, 20 November 1791, Washington Papers, series 4, reel 101; *Writings of George Washington*, 31:420.

166. Jefferson to L'Enfant, 22 February 1792, Digges-L'Enfant-Morgan Papers, box 1.

167. L'Enfant to Jefferson, 26 February 1792, 16, Digges-L'Enfant-Morgan Papers, box 1.

168. Jefferson to L'Enfant, 27 February 1792, Digges-L'Enfant-Morgan Papers, box 1.

169. Washington to L'Enfant, 28 February 1792, Digges-L'Enfant-Morgan Papers, box 1; *Writings of George Washington*, 31:488.

170. Benjamin Perley Poore, *Perley's Reminiscences of Sixty Years in the National Metropolis*, 2 vols. (Philadelphia: Hubbard Brothers, 1886), 1:54–55.

171. Thomas Digges to James Monroe, 26 October 1816, Digges-L'Enfant-Morgan Papers, box 2.

172. John Melish, *Travels in the United States of America*, 2 vols. (Philadelphia: printed for the author, 1812), 1:210.

173. Letter to the author from Thomas L. Gravell, dated March 3, 1979. Gravell is a leading authority on watermarks.

174. Commissioners to L'Enfant, 9 September 1791, Commissioners Records (RG42), Letters Sent, 1:32–33.

175. L'Enfant's probable methods of construction, as well as some of the alterations evident in the plan today, are discussed in detail in J. L. Sibley Jennings, Jr., "Artistry as Design: L'Enfant's Extraordinary City," *Quarterly Journal of the Library of Congress* 36 (Summer 1979):225–278.

176. See L'Enfant's reference to withholding his "general plan at the spot where the sale is made," L'Enfant to Lear, 19 October 1791, 3, Digges-L'Enfant-Morgan Papers, box 1; his references to the "original plan" and "the large

map,—which I had at that time in use," L'Enfant to Lear, 17 February 1792, Digges-L'Enfant-Morgan Papers, box 1; and Andrew Ellicott's statement that "Major L'Enfant refused us the use of the *Original*," Ellicott to Commissioners, 23 February 1792, Commissioners Records (RG42), Letters Received, 1:81.

177. L'Enfant to Moses Young, n.d., James Dudley Morgan, "Maj. Pierre Charles L'Enfant, The Unhonored and Unrewarded Engineer," *Records of the Columbia Historical Society* 2 (1899):125.

178. Ann Brodeau to William Thornton, 22 December 1791, John Fitch Papers, Peter Force Collection, series 8D, reel 85, Manuscript Division, LC.

179. "Observations explanatory of the Plan," [n.d.], 6 p., Digges-L'Enfant-Morgan Papers, box 2.

180. L'Enfant to Washington, 22 June 1791, 5, L'Enfant Papers.

181. William Seale, *The President's House: A History*, 2 vols. (Washington: White House Historical Association, with the cooperation of the National Geographic Society, 1986), 1:19.

182. George Walker in his broadside "A Description of the Situation and Plan of the City of Washington" (London: 1793), states that "The AREA, at the junction of the rivers, is for a FORT, MAGAZINES, AND ARSENALS." Geography and Map Division, LC, G3850 1793 .W3 Vault.

183. Jeannie Tree Rives, "Old Families and Houses—Greenleaf's Point," *Records of the Columbia Historical Society* 5 (1902):55; George S. Hunsberger, "The Architectural Career of George Hadfield," *Records of the Columbia Historical Society* 51–52 (1951–1952):57; and Federal Writers' Project,

Works Progress Administration, *Washington, City and Capital* (Washington: Government Printing Office, 1937), 878.

184. L'Enfant to Washington, [22 June 1791] Digges-L'Enfant-Morgan Papers, box 1. Version of report in handwriting of Isaac Roberdeau.

185. L'Enfant to Washington, 19 August 1791, 3, L'Enfant Papers, oversize cabinet, drawer 1.

186. John W. Reps, *Monumental Washington: The Planning and Development of the Capital Center* (Princeton: Princeton University Press, 1967), 20, footnote 28.

187. George Walker, "A Description of the Situation," Broadside.

188. *Diaries of George Washington*, 4:201.

189. George Walker, "A Description of the Situation," Broadside.

190. *Dunlap's American Daily Advertiser* ([Philadelphia] John Dunlap) (No. 4029, 26 December 1791): 1–2; *National Gazette* ([Philadelphia] Philip Freneau) 1 (no. 19, 2 January 1792):74; *Gazette of the United States* (Philadelphia: John Fenno) 3 (no. 72, 4 January 1792):286–287.

191. For a reproduction of the article appearing in the *Gazette of the United States* and a discussion of some of the differences between the manuscript plan and the newspaper account, see Richard W. Stephenson, *Quarterly Journal of the Library of Congress* 36 (Summer 1979): 216–217.

192. "A L'Enfant Memorial: Proposed Honors to the Engineer of the Federal City," *Evening Star* (Washington, D.C.) 31 May 1884, 2.

193. Claude Halstead Van Tyne and Waldo Gifford Leland, *Guide to the Archives of the Government of the*

United States in Washington, 2d ed. (Washington: Carnegie Institution of Washington, 1907), 129.

194. Public Buildings and Grounds Records (RG42), Letters Received, no. 203, 1887.

195. Ibid.

196. B. A. Colonna to F. M. Thorn, 20 May 1887. Reproduced in margin of Coast and Geodetic Survey facsimile of the L'Enfant plan published in 1887.

197. Col. C. S. Ridley to Herbert Putnam, September 26, 1918. Photocopy in L'Enfant file, Geography and Map Division, LC.

198. A. P. C. Griffin to Col. C. S. Ridley, September 28, 1918. Photocopy in L'Enfant file, Geography and Map Division, LC.

199. Ridley to Griffin, November 4, 1918. Photocopy in L'Enfant file, Geography and Map Division, LC.

200. Philip Lee Phillips to Librarian of Congress, November 16, 1918. Photocopy in L'Enfant file, Geography and Map Division, LC.

201. Ibid.

202. Richard W. Stephenson, "The Delineation of a Grand Plan"; J. L. Sibley Jennings, Jr., "Artistry as Design: L'Enfant's Extraordinary City"; and Ralph E. Ehrenberg, "Mapping the Nation's Capital: The Surveyor's Office, 1791–1818," *Quarterly Journal of the Library of Congress* 36 (Summer 1979): 207–224, 225–278, and 279–319.

203. Marian Dirda's report, January 6, 1981, 2 p., Peter Water's forwarding memorandum of the same date, 2 p., as well as treatment reports dated March 21, 1979, 1 p., September 17, 1980, 14 p., and January 22, 1985, 2 p., are in the Geography and Map Division's office files.

204. For additional information concerning the joint program, see "National Geographic Gives Grant for Project on Maps of Washington, D.C.," *Library of Congress Information Bulletin* 46 (May 18, 1987): 201–203, and Ralph E. Ehrenberg, "A Status Report on the Joint Library of Congress/National Geographic Society Washington, D.C., Map Project," *Library of Congress Information Bulletin* 49 (April 9, 1990): 135–139.

205. The original scanned data from the plan occupied twenty computer tapes, or 809 megabytes of information. Once all the unwanted background clutter was removed, however, the data for the final digitized version of the plan was reduced to two computer tapes, one for shading (105 megabytes) and one for the map itself (18 megabytes).

206. *L'Enfant's 1791 Manuscript Plan for the City of Washington: Full-Color Facsimile & Computer-Assisted Reproduction* (Washington: Library of Congress, 1991). 2 maps, each 70 × 81 cm. Accompanied by text by Richard W. Stephenson, 6 p.

INDEX

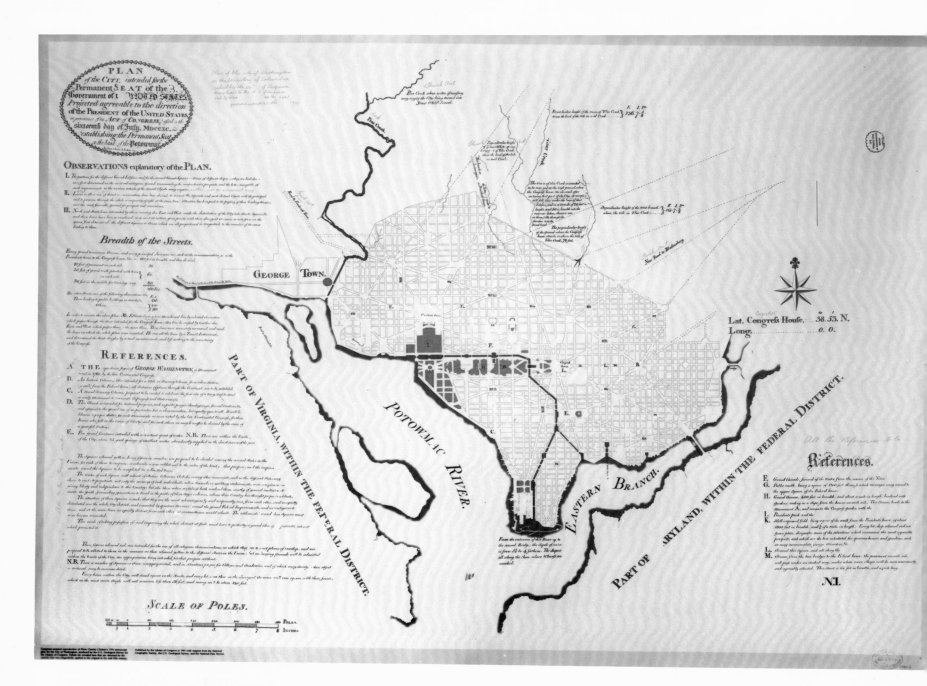